Praise for *How to Record Your Family History*

"As someone in the business of preserving memories, I've seen the emotion evoked by old photos, videos, and audio tapes of family members long gone, but not forgotten. We have young clients who spend hours, days and years digging up information about their ancestors, and spend hard-earned dollars to restore 100-year-old photos. We have had older clients who, in a race against time, spend their last years making certain their great-great grandchildren will know their stories. The biggest problem they all have is they don't know where to start. Start with this book!"

-- Penny Mannel, Owner
A Page is Turned – We Preserve Memories
www.APageisTurned.com

"I can relate to the urgency of the message of this book. Both of my parents lived interesting and valuable lives, travelled the world, and blessed thousands over the years. Unfortunately, the fascinating stories of their lives are gone. Ron Ross has written a book every person with interesting family members who have great stories to tell should buy, read and most important, apply."

-- Rich Marshall, Author/Speaker

"I just finished a video interview of my 91 year old mom --- I was amazed at the stories I had never ever heard before --- I could not have done such a good job without the help of Ron's book --- his interview questions proved invaluable to me! Thank you Ron for such insightful book! I now have a treasured possession that will continued to be treasured for generations to come!!!!"

-- Sandy Marthaler, family historian

Why I Wrote This Book

Nothing disappears as quickly as the wonderful stories of days gone by told by aging relatives. They fade away by memory loss or vanish at death.

All four of my grandparents lived fascinating lives and loved their children, grandchildren and great-grandchildren. They took seriously their roles to pass on values and wisdom developed through decades of wars and depression, trials and tribulations. But the stories and insight of how they faced challenges, overcame obstacles, won and lost, laughed and cried, and lived and faced life's end, are lost; lost forever.

That's why I wrote this book. I do not want my children and your children as well, to suffer the same sad loss.

This book is for those who see the value of preserving family history

This book was written for every person who would be overjoyed to come across an audio or video recording of an ancestor telling stories about their life and times. It was written for those who understand how family history strengthens family bonds, draws scattered family branches together, restores the connection between generations, and teaches young and old from whence they have come.

This book is for the amateur family historian

This book was written for every amateur family historian who wants an uncomplicated, straight-forward HOW TO manual that is easy to understand and apply. It is not a book of theory, but of actual practice. Everything I write about in this book I have done and continue to do on a regular basis.

The original version of the book (***Your Family History – A Guide to Preserving Family History***) now out of print, was used by thousands of family historians to preserve their family history. In this edition I updated, rewrote and added chapters to make it more useful than the original.

This book is for you

How to Record Your Family History will inspire, inform and empower you to record and preserve the fascinating, meaningful and instructive stories that presently reside in the hearts and minds of your living relatives.

For you and for the sake of your descendents, act quickly please. You know why.

Ron Ross

About The Author

Hello, I'm Ron Ross.

Most people want to know why they should trust what I say about oral history taking and preserving family history. Sounds like a fair question to me.

First of all, I've done it. In the late 1980s I set out to preserve the stories of my mom and dad's lives using a video camera (they were becoming quite popular and user-friendly back then). After many hours of research I created an oral history guide to use on Mom & Dad. Then one day we set out to record their family history starting at Dad's birthplace – Deer Trail, Colo. It took us several days and over 1400 miles of travel through Colorado, Nebraska and Iowa. The result was a family treasure: 3.5 hours on VHS video tape of their stories told in person and on location. I have done a variety of oral histories over the years.

Second, I research and write about it. Using the research I did and the experience I had with my parent's oral histories, I wrote and published a book on the subject titled, "You're Family Heritage, A Guide to Preserving Family History," now out of print. Thousands of people read the book and took action to preserve their family history, but much of the book is now out of date (It mentions arcane items such as cassette recorders and VHS tapes). This book is the updated version with a narrower focus, a more modern (digital) technology, and a new title. I continue to research, write and keep track of trends and technologies via my blog which can be found at www.RecordYourFamilyHistory. com.

Third, I lecture about it. After the publication of my first book, I was invited to lecture on the subject by the ***Colorado Historical Society*** for several years. When I spoke, they introduced me and my book to the crowd as "the seminal source for oral history taking." I've continued to speak on the subject over the years even when I didn't have an updated book to sell.

That's probably what you wanted to know when you turned to this page, but for those who like this kind of stuff, here's a brief resume:

Ronald D. Ross, B.A., M.Div., D.Th.

Ronald D. Ross is a former missionary to Africa and Christian minister who has spent much of his life traveling, writing, teaching, and as the publisher of various periodicals.

He is the Author of *Trivia Pop Quiz*, he writes a weekly newspaper column, and blogs regularly on www.RonRossToday.com. He is a Platinum Expert Author on www.EzineArticles.com, an is widely read as a contributor to www.SelfGrowth.com and other websites. He has authored several e-books on motivational and inspirational topics.

Besides writing and speaking extensively on preserving family history and other inspirational and motivational topics, Ross is the publisher of a weekly entertainment paper called Tidbits, (www.TrustTidbits.com) and he is the "Dean" of Tidbits University, the training program for all new Tidbits publishers (www. TidbitsWeekly.com).

He is the host of the weekly radio show broadcast from Colorado's oldest radio station, 1310KFKA – AM in Greeley, Colorado.

He is a husband, father, and grandfather residing in Loveland, Colorado with his wife of over 50 years.

Dr. Ross is available as a speaker on the subject of oral history or as a keynote speaker.

Email: ronalddross@gmail.com

Twitter: @ronalddross

Facebook: www.facebook.com/ron.ross

Family History Blog: www.RecordYourFamilyHistory.com (click on BLOG)

Personal blog: www.RonRossToday.com

Family website: www.RonaldDRoss.com

Dedicated to the memory of my grandparents:

ALBERT ROSS SAPP

and

NELLIE MAE SAPP

And

FRED FILMORE FILATREAU

and

IRMA OPAL FILATREAU

How To Record Your Family History

Audio – Video – Written

A practical guide to help you capture and preserve your family legacy!

By Ron Ross

www.BeaconLightPublishing.com

Published by *Beacon Light Publishing*

Denver, Colorado, USA

info@RecordYourFamilyHistory.com

ISBN: 978-0-9620144-2-0

Published in the United States of America

Contents

Acknowledgments

I would like to express special recognition and sincere thanks to the following wonderful people whose contributions helped make this project a reality:

The two people for whom this book was created - my parents, Lloyd Milton & Loretta Opal (Filatreau) Sapp, who gave me a heritage worth preserving. Several years before their deaths they allowed me to test the contents of this book on them and in the process create for my brother and me and our descendents an irreplaceable audio and video history.

My brother, Richard Lloyd Sapp, my wife of over 50 years, Amy Kay (Pickerell), and our children, David Lloyd, Jennifer Nell, and Lawrence Michael are all part of the motivation and inspiration for this book.

My favorite professor at Creighton University in Omaha, Nebr., the late Robert McEniry, S.J., Ph.D., who taught me how to listen.

Maggie, Bob, Manoj, and Julie who, by their edits, proofreading, and design expertise corrected my mistakes, improved my writing and made me look better than I deserve. Book editor Maggie Airncliffe of Ottawa, Ontario, Canada improved paragraphs, fixed clumsy sentences, and made many improvements to the original manuscript as did friend and fellow writer, Bob McDonnell of Loveland, Colo. Layout and graphic design expert Manoj Sathyavrathan of Kerala, India worked his magic touch to prepare the book for publishing on Kindle. Graphic artist Julie Beazley of Toronto, Ontario, Canada designed a most lovely book cover.

And finally, Julie Hall, The Estate Lady, who gave me permission to reprint her article, "Give the Gift of Preserving Your Family History" (Chapter 12).

Introduction

"Hey Ron, here's a copy of your family genealogy," a close friend and distant relative said, handing me a photocopy of a professionally prepared 200+ page book of our family tree. "You've gotta be in there somewhere," he smiled. I thanked him for the surprise gift and promised to cherish it.

It took a while but eventually I located my family branches. But once my initial curiosity had been satisfied, I closed the book and never looked at it again. I'm not even sure where it is today – probably in that box in the basement with all those old photographs we took from Grandma's house when she died. You know what I'm talking about because you likely have a few boxes just like it stored away somewhere for safekeeping.

An exhaustive genealogy is a wonderful thing because it lets you see how your connection to people long ago. But what a genealogical chart full of names and dates lacks is character, soul, and vitality. It's simply facts, but what many of us hunger for are the nuances and details of our ancestors' lives.

When I looked over that chart, I found myself thinking that while it was all interesting, what I would really like to know is more about the personalities behind the facts. I wondered, for instance, about the   two brothers who came here from England in the 1700s to start my family in the New World. What motivated them to leave their home for an unknown country? Why did one brother move to Chicago and the other one to Missouri? The carefully documented genealogy couldn't answer the multitude of questions I had; and it started me thinking about how sad it is that nothing had been written down or remembered about those relatives. Their personalities, contributions to the family, affect on society, unique view of life and all else are gone, irretrievably lost forever.

Think about your family tree. Wouldn't it be exciting and much more illuminating if you could know the personalities, hear the voices and enjoy the life stories of the people on that tree? Just imagine what you would do if someone handed you a video recording of your grandmother describing how her family lost everything during the Kansas Dust Bowl and what they did to survive and later prosper.

Of course, that's unlikely, because the first audio recorder (the gramophone disc) wasn't invented until the late 1800s, and the first magnetic tape recording system affordable to the masses wasn't available until 1948. Sony demonstrated the first consumer camcorder in 1980.

But things are different today; affordable, easy to operate digital audio and video devices are ubiquitous. Professional quality software for editing both digital audio and video is also available and simple to learn. So, while you will never hear your ancestors tell of their tragedies and triumphs, *your* descendants can hear and see you tell your stories. You only have to imagine for a moment how much richer your own family history would be if you could hear your great-grandfather's voice or see your three times great-grandmother's smile, to know why preserving your own stories and memories will mean the world to them.

Simply by preserving the unique voices and faces of family members still living, you can give a wonderful gift to generations to come. With a little preparation and minimal effort you can record the feelings, stories, insights, memories, opinions and wisdom of your family members in forms that transcend your written family tree. This book is designed to help you do just that. We'll guide you through everything you need to know to learn how to capture your family's stories in audio and video forms, so that the family anecdotes and memories that you treasure won't be lost and forever forgotten. This book will also show you how to document photographs and family heirlooms, so your descendants will never encounter the unanswerable questions that so many of us do as we sort through old photographs: "I wonder who that is?"; "I wonder where this photo was taken," and "I wonder what year it was?"

It is likely you have postponed taking action to preserve your family heritage, and have lost faces and voices you wish today you could see and hear again. But hesitate no longer; capture the stories of your aging relatives before your chance to do so slips away forever.

"To forget ones ancestors is to be a
brook without a source, a tree without
a root".
-- Chinese proverb

Chapter 1

Why Preserve Your Family History?

The Unraveling of Family Ties

Our fast-moving, hard-living, ever-changing culture has taken its toll on families, and in the process of daily living much of our knowledge about our personal family histories is being lost. Millions of people suffer from a sense of disconnection from their roots, and a deep uncertainty about their heritage. This is especially true for many Americans, who know little of where their family originated, what their ancestors valued and stood for, or how they came to be where—and who—they are today.

Yet we often yearn to know more about those individuals who came before us, those individuals whose very blood flows in our veins but who are, for all practical purposes, virtual strangers. This loss of a sense of our familial ties to the past is not, I don't believe, usually due to a lack of curiosity—or worse yet, sheer indifference—on our part. Rather, the reasons often lie in circumstances and events beyond our control; situations that (either singly or cumulatively) have frayed the ties that could have allowed us to remain linked to those who came before. But understanding the factors that have caused us to lose touch can also help us begin to reconstruct those braids of connection with our own histories.

The Demands of Pluralism: Fitting In

Arriving in the young, newly founded America, many immigrants were eager to embrace the opportunities and freedoms offered in the New World. To do so, however, they had to find ways to become part of the community. Understandably, many felt pressured to conform to the culture of the New World by denying both religious and ethnic roots. Wars, ethnic jokes, religious and racial prejudices and other social pressures forced some people to hide a once proud and historically significant heritage.

For instance, many immigrants, especially those of Jewish, Irish, and European descent, changed their names in order to hide their ethnic origins, thinking it would help them gain acceptance in America. Others tried to adapt to the temper of the times by emphasizing certain ethnic roots and effectively disclaiming others. During World War II, for example, a man in Colorado said his family emigrated from Russia, which at the time was an ally. After the war and with the rise of Russian communism, his parents claimed German heritage. Although in hindsight we can certainly empathize with this family's reasons, imagine how difficult it would be for descendants—who deserve to know the truth—to learn the real story of the family's history.

Hiding the Skeletons

Death, divorce, family feuds, and family skeletons can also contribute to a loss of the sense of family. A country and western singer in Texas is unable to discuss her parents with her daughter because they disowned her when she went into the music business. A man once told me he knew nothing of his family heritage. He said, "I'm just the bastard son of an L.A. whore." I knew a man with a lovely wife and two beautiful teenage children who told me his parents had never met his children because they were so disappointed that as a young man he forsook the Catholic priesthood in order to marry.

Family Mobility

Families today are mobile. Being born, living, and dying in the same village, valley, or even state may have been the norm in the past, but now it's something of a rarity. The result is often the fracturing of even the closest family ties. For example, after World War II, an entire continent separated my father and his two brothers. One lived in California, one in Colorado and the other in Florida. They seldom saw each other after the war was over.

This tendency towards mobility can cause confusion about where our own geographical roots actually are. For instance, an executive with a major corporation moved his family 17 times in 18 years. When I asked his two daughters where they were from, they looked at each other and shrugged their shoulders.

A similar thing happened in my own family. When my parents moved to Florida to retire, they wanted to be like their neighbors and erect a cute little sign in their front yard telling visitors which state they were from. But because our family had lived in several states over the years, they weren't sure which one to put on their sign.

To solve their problem they asked my brother and me, "If someone asked you where you were from, what would you say?" We both answered, "Colorado," even though for most of our lives we'd lived in other states and even other countries. So Mom and Dad erected their little sign, "We're from Colorado!" However, they could just as truthfully have said Texas, Nebraska, Indiana, or Florida itself, because they'd lived in all those places.

Resurgence

Needless to say, this sort of mobility makes it difficult for Americans to maintain ties with even our closest relatives, let alone our broader historical families. But this shouldn't discourage us, because in recent years we've seen an extraordinary resurgence of interest in rediscovering our family stories, and reestablishing family ties.

In 1976, Alex Haley published his best-selling book *Roots*, a novel loosely based on his family history. The story starts with Kunta Kinte, a boy kidnapped in The Gambia in 1767 and shipped to the Province of Maryland, where he was sold as a slave. Haley's work involved ten years of research, including travels to the village of Juffure (the place where Kunta Kinte allegedly grew up) where he listened to tribal historians tell stories of slavers. Haley found ship records which he believed documented his ancestor's journey to America. His book was published in 37 languages, and ABC-TV created a television miniseries with the same title. Haley's book and subsequent miniseries, though acknowledged as fictionalized accounts based on actual events, caused a resurgence of interest in genealogy and family history.

Interest has only grown since then, as recent searches of the two words "family history" on Amazon.com and Google demonstrates. The search on Amazon.com yielded two-million hits, and a Google search yielded over two-billion hits, which demonstrate an enormous interest in the subject created in part by TV shows like the wildly popular "Who Do You Think You Are?" The show originated in the US, but grew to include versions in Canada, Australia, and the UK, as well as the "Generations Project" produced by Brigham Young University, and the now defunct Canadian program "Ancestors in the Attic." Along with this resurgence is interest, a large variety of resources have become available for aspiring family historians, including online forums, Facebook groups, record repositories (Ancestry.com; Rootsweb.com; FamilySearch.org).

What's In It for Me?

Granted, preserving your family history can be somewhat time-consuming, and you may wonder whether it's really worth the effort. After all, those who will truly benefit are family members who may not even exist yet. But working with your family history can be as enriching for you as it will someday be for them in many different ways.

Family History is Edifying

Despite the fact that the demands of modern life often take us away from our roots, and bring out our spirit of independence, the words of English poet John Donne still ring true: "No man is an island." And nowhere does this sentiment make itself felt more than in putting together the puzzle of your family history.

Each family member is part of a larger picture that is never complete until all the pieces are fitted and in place.

You were born into a unique and intricate network of people, places and circumstances. Even though you may not be aware of your ancestors, their country of origin, cultural or religious history or the challenges they endured to bring you into the world, they have had a significant impact on who you are.

When you know your family history, it empowers you to see your life in the larger historical setting. It defines your role in the ongoing drama of life. It gives you, as Alex Haley discovered, roots.

During the mid-1980s, my parents and I were in the Silver Creek, Nebr. graveyard looking for Mom's grandparents' tombstones. She had visited the site many times as a young girl, but hadn't been there for several decades. After some wandering we found the markers and I was pleasantly surprised when I read the tombstone of her grandfather, George Washington Merrill. It revealed I was born on the same date as he was! I told Mother, "I think you should have named me George Merrill." She said, "I would have, but I didn't know you were born on his birthday!"

Family History Connects You to the Past

Something powerful happens when you discover where you came from and to whom you are connected. You realize you have ties to people you never knew existed, some who are alive today and some deceased for generations, but either way, connected by blood or marriage.

And what fun it is when you find, somewhere down the line, you are related to someone who accomplished something quite noble or for that matter, something embarrassingly ignoble. No matter what you discover, it makes a difference to who you are and who you may become.

The history we learn from school books is abstract, aloof and seldom as meaningful as a poorly written novel. But when we hear the story that our great-great-grandmother gave birth on a wagon train in a Wyoming blizzard, it makes the history of the Overland Trail and the western migration of America come to life.

Family History Can Prepare You for the Future

The more intimate knowledge you have about the lives and personalities whose DNA you share, the more you will learn about yourself. Knowing the various traits ceded to you by your ancestors can help you understand and appreciate your values, character and general outlook on life.

What you do with the genetic, personality and worldview traits they gave you is up to you. Whilst you need not be a slave to the past or the lifestyles your ancestors lived, discovering what they were and knowing them provides you tools to build your own unique life. They help you bridge the gap that separates your past from your future.

Family History Brings Families Together

Digging into family history is an interactive task that requires discussions with family members about who they are today and what they remember about days gone by. Such discussions create life-enhancing bonds across generational lines in a way that no other discussions can.

The process of family history discovery can also uncover long-lost family members. For example, if Aunt Arcella had a child out of wedlock forty years ago, that means you have a cousin out there somewhere who awaits at least your friendship and perhaps a whole lot more. There are a multitude of stories of family researchers who found relatives – even siblings – who they lived close to for decades but didn't know existed.

Family History Provides Important New Insights

Family history research opens the door to a spectrum of new insights (physical, emotional, and intellectual). At the cellular level you carry a genetic code from your family which determines such things as your height, color of hair, blood type and some personality traits. Family history preservation gives family members valuable and sometimes life-saving information about genetic traits, inherited illnesses, mental health issues, birth defects or unusual physical characteristics. It can also help answer those little puzzles, like why Uncle Joe has freckles and red hair, and everyone else is dark-haired and clear-complexioned.

A Matter of Urgency

Walk into any antique store and you will find for sale a shop full of family heirlooms lost to families who didn't care, who cared too late, or who didn't recognize the value of these items as links to their own personal past. With every death, with every estate sale, with every funeral service, wonderful stories and vital information is lost – much of it forever. And as family mobility increases and divorce disintegrates familial ties, losses accelerate exponentially.

You must preserve your family history now, before all traces of your family stories and memories disappear into dust as elderly family members pass on. For these are the things that can enliven and deepen your own understanding of your family's unique place within the world—and your own sense of belonging within it.

For instance, as grade school kids my brother and I clearly recall visiting the old family homestead on the plains of Colorado. With us were our parents, aunt, uncle and cousins, but most important, Grandma and Grandpa. On the side of the hill we could still see the scar left by the sod dugout Grandpa built and lived in while he improved the land to earn ownership. It was the same "soddy" that he'd brought Grandma to from her farm in Missouri. Not far from that spot stood a weather-worn house built for one reason - so our father would not be born in a sod house. Simply being in that place with so much historical significant for our family spoke volumes about the struggles of our grandparents to make a better life for their children, and about the continuity of our family line. But, be-

cause we were children and more interested in playing and exploring the old buildings than in listening to the stories Grandma and Grandpa told about the "old days," we also missed out on a lot of valuable insight. We were especially intrigued by a rattle-snake stuck on a plank at the bottom of a well! I also remember snippets of stories about Grandpa building the outbuildings, and a horse that escaped during a blizzard, but I didn't really listen to the details of the stories. Had I listened more closely, I would have had a greater appreciation for what my grandparents went through in that tiny two-room house on the prairie, and also a clearer sense of such a historically important time in the growth of our country. So while I gained some powerful memories of spending that day with my extended family, what was lost was the opportunity to fill in some of those little details that would have enriched my family history many times over.

But imagine how much richer my understanding of the lives and character of my courageous Grandparents would have been if I—or someone else—had recorded my Grandparents' stories before they passed on. And imagine how pleased they would have been to have been asked to sit down and record their oral history for their descendants.

What is an Oral History?

Oral histories are the oldest form of history keeping. Previous to written language, and still in tribes where written history does not exist, people re-tell the stories of their ancestors as they were told them by their parents and grandparents. The tribe or family clan preserves its heroes and remembers its moments of greatness by lovingly passing stories from one generation to the next. In some cultures, the oral history is cherished as the repository not only of a tribe or group's history but also of its collective, shared identity. Oral history depends upon human memory and the spoken word. It is limited in time with each generation, thus oral historians live in a constant state of anxiety concerned that irretrievable information is slipping from memories with each passing moment. Of course, some of this same anxiety may also be a familiar feeling to family genealogy researchers, as well!

Modern technology has made it possible for almost anyone to provide a recorded oral history for future generations, especially now when digital audio and video recorders are relatively inexpensive. Professional photography, interviewing and editing services are also available at affordable rates to help you polish your history. In fact, taking an oral history from various members of your family is one of the easiest methods for preserving your family history. In a nutshell, taking an oral history simply involves systematically collecting a person's testimony about what they experienced in their life. It is quite easy to record either a video or audio interview with a family member where significant dates, people, times, places, events, names and feelings known and experienced by the interviewee are discussed. It is not folklore, gossip or rumor, but rather, the first-hand experience and memories of the individual (although rumors passed down through generations can also be very delightful morsels, too).

Who Should Make an Oral History; and Who Should I Interview?

Everyone should create a family history! Even if others in your family are collecting family stories, that doesn't mean you can't do so as well. Each person's perspective and focus will be different, so don't be surprised if the oral history you make is quite a bit different from the one your brother, aunt or cousin makes.

And when it comes to deciding who to interview, again, the answer is "everyone." Each family member's story is worth telling and every family history is worth preserving. Each person has had unique things happen to him or her, and their life-long experiences will fascinate and inform future generations. No life has been so mundane that it does not deserve a place in recorded history.

Imagine how intrigued you would be if you found an old box in the attic that had the diary of your great-grandmother. You would read of her loves, joys, sorrows, hard times, good times, etc. If she went through disappointments, you would read of those and weep with her. If she experienced great success, you would rejoice with her. If her life was simple and mundane, you would come to appreciate her character and personality, as well as her unique perspective on her own life. Ninety years ago, as she wrote in her diary, she wasn't thinking of you, she was thinking of the events of the day. But what a wonderful gift to her grandchildren! And with each page, you would feel that much closer to a woman you never had the opportunity to know, but now have the opportunity to love.

But what if you held in your hands an oral history, and could hear her voice or see her face? What if you could hear her laugh, cry and tell stories about her childhood? Think how much more valuable that would be.

What Would You Like to Say to Your Great-Grand-children?

Chances are, you will never know your great-grandchildren. But that doesn't mean that they can't come to know you. Imagine them, at some far future time, hearing your voice and seeing your facial expressions as you describe life in the "good old days" of the year 2013. The memories, stories, experiences, and pieces of history you possess are things that only you can offer them. What an experience for them—and one that they will be able to treasure forever. And of course, don't forget to also preserve your family photos and other heirloom documents for your great-grandchildren (as discussed in the final two chapters of this book) so they will have all the resources at hand to help them get a deep and complete sense of their family heritage.

You Are Your Family's Historian

This carefully prepared and field-tested guide is designed to help you with the important task of taking oral histories from those in your family still living. What you're about to do is important! Do it with love and care.

"*People will never look forward to posterity who never look backward to their
ancestors.*"
– *Edmund Burke*

Chapter 2

Creating an Oral History

For your family members—present and future—simply having the opportunity hear and see parents, grandparents and others recount their stories will be a meaningful, fascinating experience. But a well-planned, well-executed oral history will turn your oral history into an unparalleled pleasure for your loved ones, and a treasure well worth preserving in its own right. Taking the time to plan and prepare for taking an oral history is well worth the extra effort.

There are four separate aspects that you'll need to take into account during your preparations: the interviewer, the physical arrangements, the equipment, and the interviewee/subject. When each of these three aspects are carefully prepared, not only will the process of recording your oral history flow more smoothly, but also the finished product will be more professional and polished.

Prepping the Interviewer

One of the key factors in creating an interesting, informative interview is a well prepared interviewer. In essence, as the interviewer, you will be in charge of guiding and shaping the way that the interview unfolds, both by the questions you ask, and by how you respond to what the person being interviewed has to say. Although sometimes you may find that your subject is perfectly at ease with being recorded, and will talk freely and openly without much guidance at all, at other times you may have to take a much more active, encouraging role in order to put your subject at ease.

In either case, thoughtful and careful preparation will help you to help your subject stay on track. Why is this important? Well, consider the course of a casual conversation between two people: it seems to jump from one topic to another—and even from one decade to another—quite naturally and easily. If you get confused, you can always simply ask "What year was that, again?" or "Did Jack go to the Yukon before or after the war?" But someone watching an interview doesn't have that luxury, so a story that is out of order or that jumps around may be confusing. Having a general outline of the 'shape' of the interview will help you guide the conversation in the right sequence, so that the story shines through in the best possible light.

One of the best ways to prepare is also one of the simplest: rehearse! And rehearse again, until you're comfortable in your role as interviewer. Of course, you can always rehearse alone, but recording a practice interview with a friend standing in as your subject is also a great option, because he or she may be able to offer constructive criticism that you can use to help refine your interviewing technique.   Become comfortable with yourself listening and asking questions. Practice using a conversational tone rather than reading questions. Then listen to your rehearsal tape and make any adjustments in your style that you think are needed.

Another valuable preparation tool is to watch and listen to professional interviewers. There are many TV talk and news shows and a plethora of talk radio professionals who do interviews. You'll know the good interviewers from the bad ones when you see them – imitate the good ones.

And, of course, you'll also need to come up with some great questions to ask during the interview. We've offered some examples later, but feel free to edit them to meet your specific needs. For instance, eliminate questions that you know aren't relevant and add in additional ones that are more suited to the occasion and interviewee.

Once you've prepared yourself as well as you possibly can, the only other 'prep' work we'd suggest is to relax, and enjoy the interview process; it's likely to be a one-of-a-kind experience for both you and your subject.

The Physical Arrangements

Another essential aspect of preparing to take an oral history involves thinking about the physical aspects of the interview process. This could include any number of factors, such as where the interview will take place, the amount of time involved, and any specific needs of your interviewee. In planning for each of these aspects, it is important to take into consideration a myriad of details that, unless you're aware of them, may easily be overlooked.

The length of the interview: You should allow a minimum of two hours for a simple audio interview. However, complete video Interviews can last from six to ten hours and can even take several days to complete, especially if several locations are used. For instance, when I did my parents' video history, we traveled in three states over five days to complete their story. Their audio interviews took about two hours each. The interview must be arranged in the best interest of the interviewee. Two, three or more sessions are sometimes preferred over one long taping session. Use your best judgment.

Be sensitive to the length of your interviews. Some older people (not to mention the interviewer) cannot sustain quality conversation for an extended length of time.

The time of day: The interview must be held when the interviewee is the most alert. It should also be held when the possibility of interruptions can be nearly eliminated. Don't begin an interview if you know all the cousins will be coming over at any minute, or if the rest home is soon serving lunch. Consult with your interviewee to set a good time for the interview.

The place of the interview: Two considerations should guide you in the selection of a place for taking an oral history, the comfort of the interviewee and the setting. Of first concern should be the comfort of the interviewee. The place of the interview should have comfortable chairs and access to such simple things as a glass of water and a restroom. Sit at a table if you can. Comfortable office or dining room chairs are the best as they encourage good posture which helps everyone stay more alert. Comfortable chairs are a must, but overstuffed chairs can be *too* comfortable. This not only tends to inhibit the natural body language that helps story tellers communicate openly, but may also make achieving good sound reproduction difficult.

The place of the interview should be quiet. Background noise and activity will distract you and your interviewee, making for a less pleasant experience. Not only that, but constant background noise will also be distracting, and potentially annoying, to those who will listen to the tape in years to come. Ringing telephones or constant incoming text messages, for instance, can easily disrupt the flow of your interview. If possible, arrange to unplug land lines and turn mobiles to 'silent' for the duration of the interview.

Equipment Preparations

Good recording equipment is capable of producing truly impressive sound quality, but only if you know how to use it properly. You don't have to be a recording expert to make a great quality recording, but being familiar with the equipment you're using will definitely help.

Know Your Equipment: Completely familiarize yourself with the switches, microphones and other devices that may come with your recorder. Many recorders have pause buttons, microphones switches and other features that are intended to help enhance your recording, but that may only serve to hinder your efforts if you don't have at least a working understanding of what various knobs and switches are for, and how they work. Well in advance of your interview day, practice using every feature on you recorder until you are absolutely comfortable with each of them.

It's also worth the time to give extra attention to the features you anticipate using the most during the interview. For instance, the 'pause' button can be especially useful for interruptions, coughing spells, or requests by the interviewee for a break. But use it with care, or you could end up with technical difficulties.

For clarity and consistent sound quality, two microphones are better than one; both interviewer and the interviewee should have their own microphone. If a recorder only has one input, a microphone splitter can be purchased at a radio store so that two microphones can be used. If possible, a lapel microphone is the best choice for the interviewee, because it eliminates the need for the interviewee to be face to face with a standard microphone, which can not only be intimidating but can also make the person you're interviewing feel somewhat self-conscious. Even if you checked your microphones recently, always remember to double-check their functionality just before the interview, and also do a 'voice test' for both parties so that you can double-check that each is properly set for maximum voice pick-up. You may think this is so self-evident that it's hardly worth mentioning, but you may be surprised to know how many people actually forget to do this simple last-minute check.

Some recorders have a monitor feature that allows you to hear exactly what is being recorded. You will hear the voice of the interviewee and your voice just as the tape recorder hear them.

If either voice is not heard clearly through the monitor you can make necessary adjustments.

Aside from these last minute checks and adjustments, however, try to resist the temptation to tinker with your equipment during the interview. The goal is to have your interviewee so relaxed and immersed in the experience of sharing memories and stories that they almost forget that you are recording them. Unnecessary fiddling with the equipment only serves to bring their attention back to the fact that they're being recorded, and may make them feel self-conscious or stilted.

Have plenty of recording memory on hand as you don't want to run out, and keep a clock within eyesight so that you will know when your recorder's memory is about to end.

And last, but definitely not least, use a recorder that utilizes an AC electrical outlet. Battery operated recorders should be used only if you don't have access to an AC outlet. If that's the case, however, ensure that you have an ample supply of fresh batteries on hand; how tragic it would be to lose all or parts of your oral history simply on account of weak batteries.

Helping Your Interviewee Prepare

Your main concern in arranging an oral history should always be to treat your intended interviewee with tact and sensitivity. It is likely that many of the family members you approach with a request for an oral history will be quite thrilled simply to be asked. But sometimes relatives, and especially elderly ones, may be reticent to participate because they were brought up to believe that talking about themselves was an undesirable trait. Let them know you and your family are vitally interested in all the information that resides in their memories and that your goal is to preserve the information for generations to come. Take the time to explain the meaning of what you're doing and the impact it will have on succeeding generations. This will allow them to see the value of the interview for themselves, and give them time to consider how they can contribute.

You can help your interviewee prepare further if, a few days before the interview is to take place, you give them a preview of the oral history outline you will be using. This will help them to begin thinking about their past. Also explain how the oral history will be taken and approximately how long it will take. Inform them of the recording devices and microphone.

Careful preparation of the interviewee will reduce his/her anxiety and increase their spontaneity on the day of the interview. It's also a good idea to reconfirm the date, time and place you've agreed on. And of course, never surprise your interviewee by suddenly showing up with all the equipment and paraphernalia to conduct an interview.

And of course, once the interview is underway, you'll also need to exercise sensitivity in tuning in to any concerns they have about the past, present, and future, and about things they may not want to discuss that could shed a negative light on their family history. For instance, I once did a full family history interview of a Christian pastor's mother. During the interview she avoided all mention of the pastor's father. After the interview I asked her son why she never mentioned his father. He said, "So she never mentioned him, huh? I'm not surprised." And that was the end of that conversation.

"Human beings look separate because you see them walking about separately. But then we are so made that we can see only the present moment. If we could see the past, then of course it would look different. For there was a time when every man was part of his mother, and (earlier still) part of his father as well, and when they were part of his grandparents. If you could see humanity spread out in time, as God sees it, it would look like one single growing thing--rather like a very complicated tree. Every individual would appear connected with every other."
-- C.S. Lewis

Chapter 3

Tips for Conducting a Meaningful Interview

The success and ultimate value of your oral history depends—at least partially—on the interviewer. The best oral histories are those that are taken by someone who knows how to listen not only for the facts, but also to the heart of the interviewee. While it's important to get the factual information, of course, what will give your recorded history additional depth and significance is the type of listening skills that will allow you to capture a sense of why the stories your interviewee shares with you are *meaningful* to them.

Listen With an Open Heart and Mind

You don't have to be a professional interviewer to accomplish this, but you do need to be willing to listen with an open heart and mind. The following tips will help you bring out the best in your interviewee, and make your interview go as smoothly as possible, so that both of you can enjoy the unique experience you're creating together.

1. Do everything you can to make the tape recorder and microphone as unobtrusive as possible. For instance, check your microphone and recording levels just prior to meeting up with your interviewee, so you don't need to fiddle with it once you're together. There's literally no way to make the equipment 'disappear' entirely, but being comfortable with your equipment will help put your interviewee at ease as well. Many people are intimidated by recording equipment, so before you begin the interview itself you can help your interviewee relax and become accustomed to the microphone by recording a few minutes of casual chat. Playing it back will not only let them hear their own voice (perhaps for the first time!) but will also help them get over any potential shyness at the idea of being recorded. Also ensure that the microphone is placed properly so that it catches every word they say, but is not too prominently displayed. A lapel microphone is ideal because once it's affixed it's very easy to forget it's even there. Many people who are being recorded

for the first time think that they must speak directly into the microphone at all times, which means that they may be concentrating more on their lapels than on the conversation with you. Suggest that they think of the microphone as a great grandchild sitting nearby, listening to the two of you talk.

2. Prepare your questions well in advance, so you have plenty of time before the interview to familiarize yourself with what you'd like to ask your interviewee. During the interview, try to avoid leafing through your question guide, especially while the interviewee is speaking. Remember, your prepared questions are intended to serve as a guide in the sense that they free you up from having to think up questions on the spot. The whole point of having a question guide is so that you're relaxed and able to concentrate on what your *interviewee* is saying, rather than worrying about what *you* will ask next. If you listen carefully to their answers, it's likely that you'll find that each question leads naturally to another. Ultimately, your goal is to help your interviewee feel comfortable sharing his or her memories and stories with you, so try to maintain a conversational tone rather than reading out your questions. However, always keep in mind that the central focus is your interviewee, not yourself. This means that although your aim is to maintain a conversational feel to the interview, it's best to try to limit your own contribution to the voice recording so the interviewee's personal-

ity shines through. For instance, although you will need to ask questions and clarify information, try to avoid making 'listening noises' ("uh huh" and "I see"). Instead, use a nod and a friendly smile to indicate you are listening.

3. Adhering reasonably closely to your prepared questions will usually produce a complete and fascinating oral history. But remember, you aren't married to your question guide! Be prepared for the interview to go in unanticipated directions; sometimes your interviewee may reveal something totally surprising or unexpected about your family that you never even suspected, and of course you'll want to follow that up if possible. In other words, be flexible in terms of the direction that your interview takes.

4. Of course, the interview may go in a completely unexpected direction, and get into the realm of family 'secrets' that your interviewee may want to share with you, but be reluctant to disclose for all of posterity. What do you do if the interviewee says, "Shut that stupid thing off for a minute. I want to tell you something about Uncle George."? Turn off the recorder! It's possible that your interviewee may be 'testing' you to discover whether you want certain kinds of material on tape. Let him tell you the story if he wishes to do so, and once he's finished, if you think it's a valuable piece of family history, ask for permission to record the story. If he refuses,

let it stand. After all, it's his story, and he may have good reasons for refusing. But make a mental note of the story; it may fit in at a later time in the interview when he feels more comfortable with its telling.

5. Try to frame your questions in an open-ended way that invites your interviewee to give detailed and expansive answers, rather than as yes/no questions. For example, questions like "Did you ever drive a model T Ford?" or "Did you volunteer for the military?" are 'factual' questions that are likely to get you only one-word answers. Questions that essentially ask for the details surrounding a factual event, however, invite your interviewee to share memories, feelings, and experiences along with the facts. For instance, asking "How did you learn to drive?" or "What was your first day of school like?" may unlock wonderful new insights into your interviewee's personality and character, and give your recorded history a richer, more meaningful dimension.

It's always possible, especially when you ask open-ended questions, that the interview may go in unforeseen directions, as talking about one story or memory may remind your interviewee of others. What can you do then? Again, flexibility is the key. Remember, your goal is to capture your interviewee's story and personality, not simply get through a list of questions. Try not to do or say anything that will inhibit the conversation, or the flow of information. But if you feel that the interview is seriously off track, and in danger of losing any sense of logical flow and coherency, then there are several ways you can gently guide it back to the point. In every respect try to be sensitive, compassion and patient with your interviewee.

If she rambles, you may need to interrupt your interviewee with polite questions which will re-direct the interview. For instance, you could say "You said something earlier that I would like to hear more about," or "Could we go back in time to...?" If you do interrupt, use gentle interruptive gestures such as holding the right hand up briefly with the palm out, signaling the interviewee to pause. But use this gesture very gently as it can be offensive if not used with respect.

Throughout the interview, establish a style of frequent questions. Anticipate pauses and interrupt politely. Use sentences such as: "You're getting ahead of me. Could we go back to _____ so I don't get mixed up?"

6. Don't tell your own stories. Never say, "The same thing happened to my grandmother!" Save what happened to your grandmother for *your* interview. Although your goal is to make the interview feel as conversational as possible in order to help your interviewee feel relaxed and comfortable, there is an important difference between recording an oral

40

history and having a casual dialogue with someone else. Don't forget that the reason you are conducting the interview is not to give you and your interviewee an opportunity to share your respective stories, but to collect *their* stories for future generations by capturing as much of the interviewee's personality, memories, and information as possible.

7. Ask for clarifications. If you don't understand something, it's likely that future generations will have even more difficulty understanding. Don't be afraid to ask for clarifications. "What does that mean?" "What city was that in?" "Did you say you liked it or didn't like it?" "Was that at Thanksgiving or Christmas?" "How did he manage to get it done?" This also applies to having the interviewee particularize. For instance, if they frequently use "they" or "we" or "them" you will want to get clarification of who was involved.

Another way you can ask for clarification is by asking follow up questions. Don't be afraid to probe for more information. But again, try to phrase your probing questions in an open-ended way rather than a yes/no form. "What was it like?" "How did the neighbors react to that?" "That's fascinating. Can you tell me more?" "Tell me more about that first date." Well-phrased leading questions will bring new light to the interview. When you want to avoid direct questions that might mean a moral or value judgment by the

41

interviewee, you can phrase your question so the interviewee isn't the one making the judgment. Here are some illustrations: "Did people speak well of him?" "Did most people enjoy it?" Where did other people go?" "Did the rest of the family agree?"

You may also occasionally need to clarify information for future listeners. For instance, if the interviewee gestures frequently you may need to describe the gesture since listeners won't be able to see it. When the interviewee says, "It was oh, about this long," and gestures with his hands, you can interrupt and say, "So, it was about three feet long." Likewise, the interviewee may make a pounding motion with his hand, to which you may say, "You mean he hit it with a hammer-like motion?"

Similarly, you may need to translate facial expressions for the listeners. Maintain close eye contact throughout the interview. Look at the interviewee as he/she speaks. Watch for meaningful facial expressions and translate them for the listener. Use translation phrases such as: "You're smiling." "You're frowning." "Is that a tear?"

8. Don't be afraid of silence. Silence may mean something significant is coming; give it a chance, let it come. Jumping in may prevent some very fascinating stories from coming

forth. If the interviewee is waiting for guidance from you, it will soon be clear.

9. Oral histories can be very emotional. Exploring the past can bring out anger, joy, tears, laughter, love, hate and all levels of emotion in between. So what do you do if the interviewee begins to weep? You wait. Do not turn off the recorder unless she requests it. Strong emotional expressions will have tremendous meaning for successive generations.

    Silence on your part throughout the emotional expression is usually the best reaction. Once the emotion has been expressed, you might say something like: "You feel strongly about that don't you?" "You really loved him didn't you?" "You were hurt deeply by that weren't you?" Other acceptable softly spoken sympathetic phrases are: "It's ok. Just take your time." "There – there," accompanied with a touch on the arm or hand.

    Having said that, there is certainly nothing wrong with showing empathy for what your interviewee is experiencing. If the stories you hear move you to tears or laughter, don't try to hide your own emotional responses. Laughing or crying with your interviewee is simply another way of showing them that you care.

Practical Tips for a Smooth Interview Process

1. Don't ask more than one question at a time. You want the interviewee to think carefully and logically about each question. Don't rush the interview with additional questions.

2. Don't turn the recorder on and off to save memory or to omit repetitive stories. If you do, you'll risk losing significant facts that may come out in the re-telling.

3. Allow sufficient time. Do not try to cram an entire lifetime into one 120 minute session.

4. Be aware of the clock. Your recorder will run only for the amount of time allotted. An alarm clock or other timer would be helpful. If possible, have your timer on 'vibrate' so that when it goes off, it doesn't disrupt the interviewee's train of thought.

5. Don't be afraid to take a break, especially if the interview is going longer than expected. Use the pause button from time to time to check with your interviewee as to their comfort and willingness to proceed. The Oral History Guide is designed to allow for breaks. Try to break at a memorable time in history. "Let's talk about your teen-age years after a little break, ok Grandma?"

The Golden Rule of Listening

In a nutshell, the Golden Rule teaches that we should always strive to treat others in the same way we would like to be treated. This applies to almost everything in life, including creating an oral history: listen in the same manner as you would have others listen to you. If you were giving your oral history, how would you feel if the interviewer kept interrupting, inserting his own story into the recording, or making value judgments on what you say.

I can't overstate the importance of resisting the temptation to make judgments! You may hear and learn things throughout the taking of the oral history that are surprising—or perhaps even shocking. But it's critical not only to the success of the oral history project itself, but also to the trust you are building with your interviewee, that you not express any negative judgments that may inadvertently strike you. For instance, in her oral history, an 87-year-old grandmother revealed for the first time that she intentionally got pregnant at age 17 so she could get married. The interviewer, a granddaughter, was shocked, but did not express moral judgment. She understood the trust her grandmother was showing by telling her the truth, and she also understood that her role was as the chronicler of her grandmother's life, not as her judge.

There are other ways that the temptation to make judgments may creep in, as well. Personally, you may be 'put off' by certain things such as demeanor, style of dress, offensive language or swearing, or even bad breath. But recognize these as personal prejudices that you must put aside for the moment, in the interest not only of creating a successful oral history, but also so as not to insult your interviewee.

Or perhaps your interviewee is not telling the truth, and you know it. Rather than attempt to pry the real story out of him, simply summarize what was said and repeat it back. If he sticks to the story, let it go without comment. He may have reasons of his own for keeping the true story to himself, and in this case showing respect for him means respecting the limits of what he is comfortable revealing.

Following the tips outlined in this chapter will help you create a meaningful oral history that will not only preserve a wonderful part of your family history but will also capture the vivid personality of your interviewee in a way that is sure to touch the hearts of future generations.

"The songs of our ancestors are also
the songs of our children."
--Philip Carr - Gomm

Chapter 4

Record Your Own Oral History!

Recording an oral history with another family member is always a rewarding and worthwhile undertaking, because no two people will have exactly the same perspective on experiences and events. So, interviewing more than one family member will allow you to capture a variety of different viewpoints about your collective family history. As a result, you'll create a more complete picture of your family, and a richer, more colorful record for future generations. But don't forget that you also have a unique and valuable perspective, too! Why not capture it for posterity, as well?

"Since much of the previous discussion has focused on how you can be a great interviewer, you may wonder who you could ask to perform that role while you create your own oral history. If there's someone who's interested in doing so, by all means, get them involved. But you can also record your own memories and stories without the help of an interviewer. After all, by now you should have a good idea of how the whole process works, and be adept at using your equipment, so all you need is the Oral History Guide, and several hours of quiet, undisturbed time.

You'll like find that many of the tips in the previous chapters will also apply to creating your own 'solo' oral history recording. However, there may be some differences as well. For instance, your history may contain more stories than those you do with other family members in an interview setting. That's great! In fact, the more stories the better! Try to record every story from the past that you remember, whether it is 'family lore' handed down from one generation to the next, or an incident that you personally experienced. You may be tempted to leave some stories out if you can't remember all the details. But even a small snippet of a story can be worth its weight in gold to future generations, and give insights into an ancestor's character—and often build a sense of connection with an ancestor across the years. For instance, one of my colleagues has had a special fondness for one of her female ancestors ever since she heard the story of how, during the long trip from Scotland to Canada, this woman grew so frustrated with her husband's incessant bagpipe playing that she threw the instrument overboard. My colleague cherishes this story because, tiny and incomplete as it is, it provides her with some wonderful clues about the character of her ancestors.

Be especially generous with your memories of your grandparents, great-grandparents and other now deceased relatives. You never really know what a simple story or memory will mean to someone in the future. On the other hand, try to tell your stories in a logical way, so that future listeners don't become confused about who you are talking about, and how the individual fits into your family. You can use the Oral History Guide (see Chapter 6) for tips on how to keep your story on track so that it flows in a charming way, and helps you ensure that nothing is left out.

Be personal and friendly in your telling. Pretend the recorder is a great grandchild from the 21st century who is listening in, and that your recording is your only chance to tell everything you know to this future family member. Talk about your feelings as well as the facts of the stories. If you didn't like someone, tell it like it was. If you loved someone, be sure and tell that too.

And don't be afraid to let your personality shine through. Get excited in your story telling. Describe things with colorful and lively words. Vary your vocal patterns and get involved to make your stories as intriguing as possible. On the other hand, don't get too focused on using complete sentences, or making your stories poetic.

Once spoken, go back and review what you've said. As you listen, make notes of other stories you forgot to include earlier and tell them the next time you turn on the recorder.

Recording your own oral history can be time-consuming, but you needn't complete it all at once. Give yourself plenty of time, let the memories flow, and if you become tired or need a break, take one and then come back to it when you feel refreshed. The important thing is to persevere and not quit before you feel that your family history is as complete as you can make it. Granted, creating an oral history is somewhat time-consuming, but don't let that discourage you. Remember why you're doing it. You're creating one of the most meaningful gifts of all for your children, their children, and untold future children. Time is valuable, of course, but memories are priceless.

"When I opened the box, I had to remove myself from whose handwriting
it was that I was reading and whose
story I was hearing· I had to, or I never would have made it past the first
letter· If I stopped to think about my
Grandpa writing to my Grandma, knowing how much he loved her and how
many years he spent without her after
her death, I knew I wouldn't be able to
make it through just one letter without an onslaught of tears· And it was
Grandpa, a voice I knew so well· One
that I miss terribly·" -- Kara Martinel-

li, My Very Dearest Anna

Chapter 5

An Oral History with Video

Almost everyone has a box or two of old photos stored somewhere for safe keeping that they rarely—if ever—look through. But for anyone interested in family history, these images of family members who have come before us are irreplaceable treasures. Why? If you've ever watched the TV show "Who Do You Think You Are?" you will already have a good sense of why family photos are so important. In each episode, a celebrity traces a branch of their family tree, and as they collect documents that provide the facts (names, dates, places) about their ancestors, they begin to construct a picture of what their lives were like. Yet, when they discover a photo that lets them put a face to the facts, their response is always deeply, strikingly emotional. Being able to gaze into the face of someone whose genes we carry is a very moving experience, because we literally see where we came from. This is the same impulse, in essence, that drives us to cluster around a newborn, and say "Oh, look, she has Grandma's nose," or "He's Uncle George all over; just look at those ears!" This is

the deep impulse to belong, and to recognize those who 'belong' to us in a very special way because of our family ties, no matter how distant.

As valuable as an oral history can be, recording your family history on video, so that future generations can 'meet' your interviewee 'face-to-face' will add another rich dimension to the experience for future generations, especially once your interviewee has passed on.

Creating a video oral history does demand careful planning, creative imagination, and good camera skills (or willingness to learn) but it is well worth the extra effort! The quality of the end result will depend, as it does for audio recordings, on how well prepared you are. In this chapter, you'll find a number of general guidelines and ideas that will help you produce a wonderful video about your family history. Of course, providing you with specific instructions on how to use your camcorder is beyond the scope of this book, but we suggest that you consult your user's manual and familiarize yourself with the basic operations and functions of your camera before you embark on something as important as your family history.

Preliminary Questions

Just as importantly, there are a number of questions that you'll need to ask yourself at the pre-planning stage, in order to ensure that your video recording session is as successful as possible. Here are a few things to consider:

1. Is the interviewee you have in mind a good prospect for a video interview? Is he or she willing to be on camera? If so, will your interviewee 'play' to the camera in an interesting way? In other words, will he or she act naturally and spontaneously when the camera is on, or be distracted or intimidated by its presence?

2. Do you have the kind of equipment (camera, lights, microphone, etc.) that will produce a quality video?

3. Are you confident enough in your skill level with your equipment, or would you be more comfortable having some-

one else take over the videotaping duties on your behalf? If you're not confident in your skills, would a little more practice do the trick? Or, is there a class or course you might enroll in that would help polish up your skills?

Digital Video Equipment

Once you've answered these questions honestly, there's one more question that you need to ask yourself. How important is it to you to produce a polished, professional-looking video?

If your aim is to create a high definition video that will look just as great as professional movies, you can invest in an HD camcorder. Currently, you can expect to pay anywhere between $200 and $1500, depending on the features you choose. Because technology changes so rapidly these days it would be impossible for this book to offer recommendations with respect to which camera to purchase. In addition, prices on HD camcorders keep coming down as the quality of the images they produce keep improving. But with a little research and comparison shopping on your part, you'll find the right camera for your needs.

However, don't think that you absolutely must spend a bundle, and then invest in training to learn to use your equipment before you are able to make a good quality video recording. If professional quality if one of your main concerns, but you don't want to invest upwards of a thousand dollars on equipment, you may also want to consider renting a camcorder, or hiring someone to do the actual filming. When I did my parents' family history, I opted to rent the best video camera I could, but do the filming myself. This was several years ago, and by today's standards the quality might be considered less than perfect, but nothing can lower the quality of the memories we captured, and to me, that was the most important point of creating the video history.

Getting the Best from Your Equipment

Whichever way you decide to go with respect to camera equipment, if you do opt to shoot the video yourself, there are a few things to keep in mind that will help you get the best results. For one thing, if at all possible, shoot your video using a tripod. Hand-held videography is difficult even for skilled professionals. A tripod allows you to frame the shot and then enjoy hands-free recording.

Most camcorders are very good at automatically adjusting for light. Your goal in lighting is to be able to see the face or other objects of importance clearly. Work to eliminate harsh shadows and white hot spots. Check your owner's manual for further lighting suggestions. Experiment with lighting until you have a visually clear and colorful picture. Take the time to get it right. Video experts suggest back lighting, side lighting and other techniques for maximum results.

Sound reproduction is absolutely vital. If you use the mounted external microphone (the one attached to your camcorder), you must always be as close to the interviewee as possible. Be aware that on-camera mikes do not allow for much camera action. Another aspect of sound quality that many people overlook is background noise. Eliminate as much background sound as you can: close the doors and windows, and turn off phones, radios, televisions or any other device that might distract your interviewee—and future viewers.

Power the video camera with the AC connection if possible. If you must use batteries make sure they are fresh and that you have an extra supply not only for your camera but also for all your camera's accessories as well.

Plan Your Production

The simplest way to produce a video history is to have Grandma sit down, hook a microphone to her, turn on the lights, point the camera at her and tell her to talk about the olden days. If Grandma is a "ham" and is not intimidated by all the equipment, you will get a few interesting shots. However, you can usually create a more interesting video history if you plan out the interview and 'script' the production, at least loosely. One way to do this is to talk over the interview in advance with your interviewee and an advisor, if you have one. This gives you an opportunity to discuss the topics you'll cover with your interviewee before taping begins, so that they aren't taken by surprise about certain aspects of your questions.   Both the interviewee and the interviewer should have a good idea about what direction the taping session will be moving in. Start by using the Oral History Guide in this book, but much more can be done if you use your imagination and plan ahead.

Creative Tips from the Experts

You can make your video history even more interesting and meaningful by using your own imagination to add color and excitement. Here are a few tips from the experts to get your creative juices flowing.

1. If you have a family album, bring it along to the interview, and film your interviewee leafing through the pages and talking about the various people and events. Add the photos to your video itself during the editing process to give viewers a sense of being involved in the process. Having these photos at hand will not only help trigger your interviewee's memory, but will also give them something to focus on besides the camera. Another way to accomplish this is to select individual photos that are meaningful to your family, and mount them on plain dark cloth or on a wall. Invite your interviewee to talk about each one, and capture the photos with your camera as she does so.

2. Important family documents such as birth certificates, wedding licenses, military medals, diplomas, can also help stimulate stories and memories.

3. Invite your interviewee to bring along important personal items such as silver, paintings, antiques, furniture, clothing, or other family heirlooms and talk about them. Use various camera actions such as zooming, tilting or panning as the interviewee speaks.

4. Drive to the old homestead and take videos while the interviewee recalls life there. Find the tree where Grandma had the swing, or the place where Grandpa first worked and video there. Even if these places are now vacant or have been re-built into something different, being there will help the interviewee's recall and make the video history more interesting.

5. Play Grandma's favorite music while she talks about it. Take her to the old school grounds, the church she attended, or the park where she played as a child, let her tell stories and describe the places as she remembers them. Take a drive through town and let Grandma talk about her experiences of the home, streets, stores, etc.

6. A graveyard where family members are buried can also be an interesting filming location. Have the interviewee read tombstone inscriptions and recount any memories or stories she has about the people buried there. (Be sure and note the location of the graveyard in the taping, as well as any grave numbers if available.)

7. Have the interviewee talk with other old timers (brothers, sisters, old classmates, war buddies, etc.) and recall memories.

8. Go to the church where the interviewee was married to have him/her talk about the wedding, who was there, and anything else they can remember about their special day.

Use as many visual aids and various locations as possible. But note, each visual aid you use, and every different location, will pose different technical requirements. In order to ensure that everything goes as smoothly as possible during the actual taping, it's a good idea to experiment and rehearse with your equipment before you bring the interviewee into the session. That way you can resolve any technical problems before you begin taping.

What to Wear?

Ask your interviewee not to wear white, as it can 'wash out' on camera. Also, busy patterns (plaids, stripes, or fancy/bold prints) can be very distracting and hard to film, so suggest that your interviewee choose soft pastel colors instead.

The Four Critical "DOs"

1. Plan. Despite your best intention, without careful planning the chances are high that you won't complete your video history. It is very easy to get off-track, become discouraged, or run into problems that you didn't anticipate. Careful plan-

ning allows you to resolve any potential issues in advance, so your filming day goes off smoothly and without any unexpected glitches.

2. Rehearse. Practice the various techniques you wish to employ. Solve all technical problems before you bring the interviewee into the taping session. Know where you're going. Know what you're doing. This can only come from rehearsals.

3. Take your time. A video history cannot be rushed. Each sequence will take time and effort. Inform the interviewee that the taping sessions will take time. And above all, be sensitive to their energy limits.

4. Edit. For the best possible video history find an editing studio which will help you edit your footage into one final production. There are many home-based video editors available to help you at a reasonable price.

A request from the author: I would dearly love to hear from you, and with your permission, share your video histories, as well as your successes and challenges along the way, with other readers. Sharing your knowledge just may help someone else get over or through a hurdle they're facing with their own family history. Or you may find a solution to one of your own. So, please don't hesitate to get in touch with me through: www.RecordYourFamilyHistory.com.

"We all grow up with the weight of history on us· Our ancestors dwell in the attics of our brains as they do in the spiraling chains of knowledge hidden in every cell of our bodies·"

-- Shirley Abbott

Chapter 6

Oral History Guide

Introducing Your Family Record

As the interviewer, it is your responsibility to make some sort of formal introduction to the oral history you create in order to give viewers the background and context they will need to get the most out of your family history. In particular, it is important to mention the date, place(s) and names of the people involved. Your introductory remarks may sound something like this:

"The date is Sunday, June 23, 2013 and I am William Andrew Beeson. I am very pleased to be interviewing my grandmother,

Mildred Ruth Campbell Beeson. The interview is being conducted in her apartment at the Sunrise Senior Living complex located in Montgomery, Alabama. Helping us out with the video camera is my daughter and namesake of Grandma Beeson, Sarah Ruth Beeson."

Oral History Guide

Part I. General Family Memories

Although in the end you are aiming for a free-flowing interview rather than something that feels stilted or overly scripted, I strongly suggest that you begin your interview by asking about the interviewee's closest personal history. There is an important reason for this: it is almost always easiest for folks to talk about the things they are most familiar with, such as their parents, siblings, and home life. Being able to easily answer the questions you pose about their own history allows them to relax, which in turn will help stir their memories and give you an unforgettable interview. If you feel that it's appropriate, ask for more details with the use of open-ended questions, such as "Can you tell me more about that?" "What happened after that?" and "Help me to understand…" But remember, not every question that's included in this guide will be relevant to the person you are interviewing, so use your own discretion.

- Give the specifics of your birth
  - Full name
  - Date and place of birth
  - Conditions surrounding your birth (weather, season, etc.)
  - Your health at birth
  - Your mother's health at your birth

- o   What stories were told about your birth?
- Memories of your mother

  - o   Her maiden name
  - o   Birth date and place
  - o   Her parent's names, birth dates and birth places
  - o   Her brothers and sisters, physical characteristics, talents
  - o   Describe her personality, what made her happy, what made her sad
  - o   Describe her role in the home?
  - o   How was she treated by other members of her family?
  - o   Did she have strong opinions? For instance, what did she think about religion, politics or social life?
  - o   What did she like to do best?
  - o   What was she like as she aged?
  - o   Tell a favorite story about your mother
  - o   If deceased, what were the circumstances of her death?
  - o   Date, place and place of burial of your mother

- Memories of your father

  - o   His full name
  - o   Birth date and place
  - o   His parents' names, birth dates and birth places
  - o   His brothers and sisters, physical characteristics

- How did he earn a living?
- What were his gifts and talents?
- Describe his personality, what made him happy, what made him sad?
- What was his role in the home?
- How he was treated by other members of his family?
- Did he have strong opinions? For instance, what did he think about religion, politics, or social life?
- What did he like to do best?
- Was he ever in the military?
- What did he do in retirement?
- Tell a favorite story about him
- If deceased, what were the circumstances of his death?
- Date, place and place of burial of your father

- Memories of siblings
  - Name your brothers and sisters - Give full names, birth dates and places of birth
  - Describe each one's physical characteristics
  - Describe their personalities
  - What made each one unique?
  - Any favorites?

- ○ What has been your relationship with them as the years have gone by?
- ○ Are they still living? Where?

● Memories of living at home

- ○ What rules did your parents have for the children?
- ○ Did your parents usually agree on how to raise the kids?
- ○ To whom did you go for a special request?
- ○ What chores did the children have around the house?
- ○ How were you punished for doing wrong?
- ○ How do you feel about the way your punishment was administered?
- ○ Talk about family meals – frequent, fun, formal
- ○ Who did the dishes?

● More memories about your parents

- ○ How did your parents get along with each other?
- ○ How did they face adversity?
- ○ Did your father help out around the house?

● Family visitors

- ○ Did you have many visitors in your home?
- ○ Who? How long? Why?
- ○ Any real special visitors? Who? Why?
- ○ Any long staying visitors? Why?

Oral History Guide

Part II. Memories of Stories Told

The purpose of this section is to help your interviewee reach back into their memories to re-tell stories they heard about their ancestors. The idea is to retrieve stories told by deceased family members and thus fill in the gaps of family history. Inquire about all grandparents, great grandparents and great-great-grandparents. Use such questions as, "Can you remember anything else your Grandmother said about that?" and "What else do you remember hearing them say?"

Introductory comments to this section might be something like this: "Members of your family sure would like to have recordings like this of your parents and grandparents. Since they are gone, I'm going to ask you to go back in your memory as far as you can to recall stories you heard about your grandparents and other relatives who have gone before you and recall them for your descendants."

● What are your earliest memories of your grandparents?

  ○ Describe your grandparents' physical characteristics

  ○ What customs and traditions did you observe with them? Holidays, birthdays, foreign languages, etc.

  ○ Do you remember their home?

- o   Do you have any treasured family heirlooms? Describe them. Where are they?

- o   Was religion important to your grandparents?

- o   How did they practice their religion?

- Go back even farther in your memory to recall stories you heard about your grandparents or great-grandparents.

- o   Immigration stories, "Old Country" stories, famous ancestors, any family skeletons you feel brave enough to reveal?

- o   What about other great-aunts or great-uncles or other now deceased relatives you personally remember or you remember hearing about? Name them and describe them, tell any interesting stories about them.

- o   Did any one of them have a particular influence in your life?

Oral History Guide

Part III. Childhood Memories (Ages 5-12)

When you're ready to move forward in time with your inter-viewee, make a few introductory remarks to let them know that you're changing directions. You may say something like this, "You have already told about your birth. So let's move forward in your life and talk about some of your childhood memories."

- What are your earliest childhood memories?
  - Special toys
  - Special playmates
  - Share as many memories of your childhood as you can

- School days
  - Describe your first school house
  - Tell us about your grade school teachers?
  - How did you get to school?
  - Did you like school?
  - Did you participate in athletics?
  - Tell about your special elementary school friends

- o Did you have any elementary school achievements worthy of note?

- o Funny or sad things that happened to you during elementary school

- What are your childhood memories of relatives (uncles, aunts, cousins, etc.)?

  - o What animals/pets did you have in your childhood days?

  - o What were your favorite games?

  - o What else did you do for fun?

  - o Do you remember any favorite sayings, songs, rhymes, poems, etc.?

  - o What about favorite childhood clothes?

  - o Were you forced to wear anything you didn't like?

  - o What fads do you recall?

  - o Did you have any heroes? Who did you look up to?

  - o What jobs/chores around the house were your responsibilities? How did you feel about doing them?

  - o Any childhood hobbies?

- Let's talk about family activities

  - o What were some of the fun activities you did as a family?

  - o What about family difficulties during your childhood? Financial, health related, deaths, accidents, divorce

- ○ How was religion practiced in your home?

- ○ Describe any childhood religious experiences

- ○ Any special vacations or trips?

- ○ Thrilling experiences (clubs, personal adventures)

- ○ Anything else?

- ○ Unusual happenings, special people, life-changing events

Oral History Guide

Part IV. Teenage Memories (Ages 13-19)

Another transitional sentence would be appropriate to introduce the teenage years. Again, your remarks can be quite brief; perhaps something like this, "It sounds like you had a very interesting childhood. Let's talk now about your teenage years."

- Describe yourself as an early teen

- What were some of the things you dreamed of as a teenager?

- Describe the school/s you attended as a teen

  - Buildings
  - Teachers
  - Others

- What were your favorite classes?

  - Least favorite?
  - Grades?

- Other school activities

  - Sports
  - Clubs
  - Troubles
  - Honors

- ○ Any now famous classmates?
- ○ Have you been to any reunions?
- What about your teenage social life?
  - ○ Dances
  - ○ Movies
  - ○ Music
  - ○ Dating
  - ○ Outings
  - ○ Summer/winter activities
- What kinds of things were you absolutely not allowed doing?
- Describe the clothing styles of your teenage years.
- What jobs did you have?
  - ○ How much were you paid?
- Did you travel any as a teenager-either with or without family?
- Any significant adventures or misadventures?
  - ○ What did you do to get into trouble?
  - ○ What did you do to get out of trouble?
- What was your role around the house?
- What kind of things did your parents say about you?
- Did your family have any pet names for you?

- Besides your parents, who had the greatest influence on you in your teenage years?

- What about religion in your teenage years?
  - Attendance at religious services
  - Any significant religious experiences?
  - Religion classes, youth groups, etc.
  - Any important religious people in your life (pastor, priest, Sunday school teacher, rabbi, etc.)?

- Tell us about your earliest romance
  - First person of the opposite sex you really liked
  - First date
  - First broken heart
  - Other romantic experiences

- Describe the fads of your teen years
  - What did "everybody" do?
  - Fashions, entertainment, sports, music idols
  - What did old people say about teenagers when you were one?

- Recall the people in the news and other significant national and international events of your teen years.

- Military service

  - Branch
  - Reason for entering, basic training, special training
  - Type of duty
  - Special buddies
  - Leisure activities while in military
  - Travel
  - Conflicts
  - What did you like / dislike about military life?
  - What did you learn about life while in the military?
  - Honors or medals?

- College or Technical School

  - Where did you attend?
  - Why?
  - How financed?
  - Where did you live while in college?
  - Special friends of the same sex
  - Romances
  - Subjects studied, major interests
  - Special activities
  - Social life, dating

o   Influential professors

o   Honors, achievements, degrees

o   If dropped out, why?

o   Conflicts

o   Important decisions

o   Any other interesting items about your college days

Oral History Guide

Part V. Courtship and Marriage

The subject of courtship and marriage can be a sensitive one if, for instance, a spouse has passed on (especially very recently) or if a marriage ended in divorce or separation. Regardless, many people have particularly strong and emotional memories about this area, so both tears of sorrow and joy can suddenly flow. Listen carefully and give your subject time to respond. Silence sometimes is needed, but don't be quick to shut off the recorder. It can be the gateway to some wonderful comments.

- When did you first meet your spouse?
  - First impressions
  - First date
  - Special dates
  - Lover's spats
- Tell about your engagement
  - How was the question "popped"?
  - Marriage preparation, showers, pre-nuptials
  - Anything special or unusual happen during your engagement?
- The wedding
  - Date, time, place
  - Pastor or other officiate

- o Special circumstances and arrangements

- o Music and musicians

- o Wedding party (names of all who participated, colors, decorations, etc.)

- o Humorous or unfortunate happenings

- o Any other interesting or noteworthy things that happened.

- Honeymoon

  - o Where?

  - o What kind of transportation?

  - o What did you do?

- Your in-laws

  - o First impressions

  - o Their impact on your marriage, helpful/hindrance

- Let's talk about your mate

  - o What most attracted you to your mate?

  - o Describe his/her personality

  - o What were you greatest challenges as newlyweds?

  - o Where did you first live after your wedding? Describe the place as thoroughly as you can.

  - o Describe your first meal

  - o First guests in your home

  - o Other interesting anecdotes of your early marriage

Oral History Guide

Part VI. Married Life

This section focuses on your interviewee's married life in general, while the next section focuses on children. Of course, your interviewee may want to wander off into stories about children, since they are often a very big part of a couple's relationship. If that happens, you have two choices. You can gently interrupt and say, "We're going to spend plenty of time talking about your children in a moment, but right now let's talk more about your marriage." Or you can let them tell their story, children and all!

- How did you get what might be termed as "settled down"?

- What kind of problems did you have making ends meet?

- Agreements – disagreements as a married couple?

- What was your role in the home?

- Employment or career

  - How selected

  - Changes

  - Promotions

  - Transfers

  - Failures – successes

  - How much did you get paid?

  - Impact of job on family

o How did you feel about your job?

o Tell how your job was done- special tools or tasks

o Membership in unions, business or professional organizations

o Unusual job experiences

Oral History Guide

Part VII. Married Life and Children

Most parents naturally like to tell stories about their children, and memories of our children's growing up years can be especially strong and detailed. Ensure that you give your interviewee sufficient time to talk about their children. Take a break if necessary. Praise and encourage your story teller as you progress! Again, use a short transitional sentence when you begin asking about your interviewee's children, to let them know that your focus is shifting.

- In their order of birth, tell about each of your children

  o Full name and its significance

  o Date of birth, place of birth

  o Health of mother and child at birth

  o How did your partner handle the birth?

  o Special circumstances of the birth

  o Special characteristics of each child, talents, hobbies, special interests, cute sayings, stories of their growing up

  o Problems of parenting

  o Your children's special achievements, honors, joys and sorrows.

- Family Life. "Now let's talk about family traditions and how you celebrated holidays and special occasions in your home.

84

I'm going to mention a few, and I'd love it if you could tell me what you remember about each one."

- ○ Birthdays
- ○ Christmas
- ○ 4th of July
- ○ Thanksgiving
- ○ Halloween
- ○ Memorial Day
- ○ Graduations
- ○ Baptisms or similar religious services
- ○ Mother's Day
- ○ Father's Day
- ○ Weddings
- ○ Valentine's Day
- ○ Other special family days
- Tell about some of your favorite family vacations
- How was religion practiced in your home?
  - ○ How did you feel about it?
- What sort of influences changed your family patterns either for the good or for the worse? (Depression, wars, death, divorce, success, failure, etc.)

- What were some of the general guidelines you lived by as you raised your family?

- Tell about your children as they grew up and left home.

  ○ College, marriage, jobs

  ○ Special achievements

  ○ Their children (your grandchildren), great grandchildren, great- great-grandchildren

  ○ Where are they now? What are they doing?

Oral History Guide

Part VIII. Married Life- The Middle Years

Make sure your subject understands that the following questions relate to married life after the children grew up and left home. Again, use an appropriate transitional sentence to introduce the section.

- How did your life change as the children left home?
  - More money, new jobs, changing interests
- Health of you and your mate
- Things you enjoyed
- Favorite food
- Favorite place to go
- Best friends
- Favorite clothes
- Favorite music, musicians, movies, movie stars
- Who were your heroes or role models?
- Describe the home/s of your middle years
- Describe the community of your middle years
- Civic and political activities

- o   Clubs, fraternities, lodges, etc. positions held, services rendered, honors earned
- o   Political affiliation
- How did your religion impact your middle years?
  - o   Church affiliation
  - o   Positions held
  - o   Attendance pattern
  - o   Important spiritual events
- Any business ventures?
  - o   Describe their success or failure
  - o   Impact on your middle years
- Memorable travels
- Important national and international events you remember
- Comment on how your family changed in your middle years
  - o   Marriages, divorce, death, etc.
- Other significant events, achievements
  - o   Joys, sorrows, disappointments
  - o   Causes for celebration

Oral History Guide

Part IX. The Retirement Years

A good way to introduce this section is for you to give a brief overview of the subject's life. You might, for instance, say something like this, "Wow, Grandma Beeson, you have had a full and remarkable life. This has been very interesting. Let's talk now about your retirement years, okay?"

● Describe your feelings as you approached retirement.

● What impact did retirement have on you?

○ Financial condition

○ Special moves, difficult adjustments

● What's been the best part of retirement?

○ New friends

● What's been the most difficult part?

○ Health

○ Finances

○ Funerals

Oral History Guide

Part X. Pride and Wisdom

This can be the most meaningful part of your entire interview because everyone loves to feel that the wisdom they are able to pass on is both sought and valued. Don't be surprised, then, if this is the section of your oral history that really brings out the personality of your interviewee.

Your transitional sentence might sound something like this, "Grandma, it sounds to me like you have so much to be proud about, and you have so much wisdom to pass on. The children of your grandchildren will never have a chance to know you in person, but I'd like to ask some questions about what you'd like them to know about you, if you could talk with them right now."

Pride

- Your two or three most significant personal accomplishments (more or less is ok)

- What have your family members (parents, mate, children, grandchildren, etc.) done that is a source of pride for you?

Wisdom

- How do you stay healthy?

- What significant values have guided you through life?

- How does your religion help you now?

- Memories we've discussed that bring you joy

- Memories we've discussed that bring you sorrow

- Summarize what you think gives meaning to your life

- How do you want people to remember you?

- Many of your descendants will likely listen to this tape. What advice would you give them about life and living?

- Any other words of wisdom that you've learned and would like to share with your descendants

- Have you thought about an epitaph?

- Any special instructions for your funeral?

- Any final words?

Concluding Your Interview

End the session with a statement similar to the opening statement. "We have been talking with 87-year-old Mildred Ruth Campbell Beeson at her apartment in the Sunrise Senior Living Complex located in Montgomery, Alabama. The date is Sunday, June 23, 2013, and I am William Andrew Beeson, her grandson. Helping us has been my daughter and namesake of Grandma Beeson, Sarah Ruth Beeson. Grandma Beeson, we love you and thank you for telling us your life story!"

"*Every book is a quotation; and every house is a quotation out of all forests, and mines, and stone quarries; and every man is a quotation from all his ancestors.*" -- Ralph Waldo Emerson

Chapter 7

**Editing, Transcribing, and Publishing
an Oral History**

All About Editing

Make Copies! Both audio and video recordings should be edited for easier listening/viewing. However, before any editing is done, *create several duplicates* of the original raw recordings and store them in two or three different locations for safety's sake. In many cases, they will not be replaceable. Equally important, *never* edit any original audio or video recordings in order to maintain the integrity of the originals. Edit only the copies you've made. Of note, copying digital files does not result in quality loss like the duplication of the old magnetic tapes, so make as many copies as you like.

Audio Editing Resources

With a little effort you can learn to edit audio files like a pro. An easy-to-learn, professional quality, and absolutely free audio editing and recording resource called Audacity is available online at Audacity.sourceforge.net. Audacity is an open source, cross-platform software for recording. A variety of free tutorials can be found on YouTube.

If you prefer, you can hire someone to do your editing. Professional audio editing and enhancing services are available at various prices; simply search online for "audio editing services," and you'll find a variety of websites to peruse.

Video Editing Resources

Video editing requires more skill and technical knowledge than audio editing does. Even so, easy to learn and moderately priced software (some free) does exist. There are many home-based business men and women who do video editing for bargain rates. Use your favorite Internet search engine to search "video editing services + (your town)," and you'll likely find that someone nearby is in the business!

Ideas for Audio Editing

Things you can (and usually should) edit out of your audio recording:

- Opening noises such as those created by fiddling with microphones, sliding of chairs, shutting of doors, etc.

- Interruptions. Ringing phones, people coming and going, technical problems

- Excessive bad language (though this will seldom happen)

- Lengthy and meaningless comments by the interviewer. It's easy for an interviewer to want to make the recording a dialogue by telling their own stories. Unless those ramblings are relevant, they should be edited out.

- Extended coughing or repetitive throat clearing

Things you should *not* edit out:

- Laughter and tears

- Sighs, groans, laments

- Some bad language compatible with the storyteller and his/her stories is acceptable

Things you can edit in:

- Introductory remarks can be expanded to clarify any confusion, identify all participants and declare time, place and date. Brief (10 second) musical transitions with voiceovers placed strategically between sections can be easily edited into an audio recording. Example: A ten-second musical transition with an accompanying, "Next Grandma Beeson will talk about her days as a youngster living on the farm outside of Montgomery, Alabama. "

Ideas for video editing

With video editing you have much more flexibility to create an interesting family history.

You can add titles and music to the beginning and end, titles and subtitles throughout the video, overlay historic photos and documents, and make interesting video transitions with headlines that identify each section. You can even add corrective subtitles such as, "Grandpa meant to say Vietnam War."

Duplicate all recordings multiple times

Use family photos to create colorful covers for your CD and DVD disks and boxes. Be sure to include names and dates on the covers. Then for posterity, make multiple copies using quality discs and professional services if possible.

Transcribing Your Oral History

You will expand the usefulness and value of an oral history by transcribing your recording. Although this can be a labor intensive and time consuming task, it is well worth the effort because it is another very useful way to document and preserve your family history.

If you don't want to transcribe the recordings yourself, use a professional transcribing service. Search "transcription services" on the Internet and you'll have several options. However, if you're keen to give transcription a try yourself, here are some tips that will help make the task easier and more rewarding.

Transcribe the Interview Verbatim—and Accurately

The central point of transcription is to put the whole interview into written form *exactly* as it was spoken. This is not the time to show off your creative editing skills! Include all sounds as well as all spoken words on the recording just as they occur—and in the precise order in which they occur. Careless or inaccurate transcription can result in a dramatic distortion of the original meaning. The following example illustrates how transcribing all the words, but not in the right order, destroys accuracy by drastically changing the meaning:

As he left, he threw momma a kiss from the train.

He threw momma a kiss as he left from the train.

He threw momma from the train as he left from the kiss.

Which is correct? If all a future member of your family has to go on is the transcription, what your interviewee actually said—and meant—is likely to forever remain a mystery. And in that case, putting in the time and energy to make a transcription in the first place is futile.

Convey the Conversational Quality

Another task of the transcriber is to convey the personality and individuality of the speaker. When we speak, we are less accurate about grammar and sentence construction than when we write. This means that as the transcriber, you may have to invent some new forms of punctuation and spelling in order to capture the oral quality of the words. Incomplete sentences, indistinct paragraphs, and phonetic spellings will all be a part of the verbatim.

If the speaker says "we ain't those kinda folks" or "we just threw a couple of cobs on the stove and *het* (heated) it up… that's how we got warm… ya see," then that's how it must be transcribed.

Sometimes clarity demands more than just a pure transcription. When this happens, you can do one of three things:

1. Your first and most frequent way is to use phonetic spelling and creative punctuation to make sure the message gets through.

2. Use italics (or underline) to indicate the intentional misspelling and follow the misspelling with the correct word in parentheses (note previous paragraph).

99

3. Footnote the correct spelling with additional explanations

Contractions should usually be used as spoken. However, it is not necessary to intentionally and consistently misspell words to reflect a particular dialect or ethnic background. The transcriber could spend hours inventing contractions and new spellings. If you run into situations like this, use your own discretion. After all, the point of transcribing the interview is to preserve it for future generations, so clarity is something better than inventiveness.

Pausing, Crutch Words, Stammering, and False Starts

Guttural pausing words (e.g. "uhhhh" and "errr") are not necessary to include in the verbatim. However, if the sounds express surprise, sadness, or other emotion (e.g. "Oh, yea, oooooh wowwie"), include them.

Guttural sounds meaning yes and no (e.g. "u-huh" and "huh-a") should be translated as "yes" or "no."

Pausing, crutch words and phrases (e.g. "ya' know" and "anyway") can clutter up a verbatim and make reading difficult, yet they are a part of the speaker's speech pattern. Transcribe them all.

Stammering and stuttering, on the other hand, need not be transcribed.

Speakers often begin a sentence then start over before the first sentence is complete. This is called a false start. For instance, someone may say, "Oh, yes, I was a sickly... Well my mother said all us kids was healthy 'cept me, yes I was the sickly child." Most oral historians suggest transcribing false starts and repetitions. Some false starts and repetitions may have to be deleted for the sake of clarity. However, delete as little as possible.

Emotions

Laughter, weeping and other expressions of emotions should be noted in the verbatim with a parenthetic comment. No capitalization or periods are necessary.

Examples:

"When the horses (laughter) were finally put back in the corral (laughter), we were all worn out..."

"My little baby brother died in my arms (sobbing). There wasn't a thing I could do (weeping)."

Other Sounds and Actions

Speakers will clap their hands, pound the table, and perform other actions that need to be described for the reader. Describe all sounds and actions with a parenthetic statement as shown in the previous paragraph.

Punctuation

Punctuate for maximum clarity. Utilize existing rules of punctuation whenever possible. When in doubt, consult an editor's style manual for accuracy. The most commonly used style manual is Strunk & White's "The Elements of Style."

Tone of voice, excitement, and emphasis can be conveyed through use of an exclamation point. However, be aware that overuse of the exclamation point reduces its meaning.

While the comma is the usual punctuation mark used to denote a pause, the transcriber can also use the em dash (–). The em dash is properly used to mark a suspension of the sense, a faltering speech, a sudden change in the construction or an unexpected turn of the thought.

Example: "It was my first airplane ride – not for the rest of them – but it was my first."

Three points of ellipsis (…) are used to indicate an omission, a lapse of time, or a lengthy pause.

Example: "Momma saw the Indians coming, and she didn't know if they were friendly or hostile…she was scared…we were all afraid for our lives."

Three points of ellipsis can also be used at the end of a sentence to indicate that the interviewee trailed off without finishing the thought.

Example: "Dad worked on the railroad, but times was hard, so..."

The Interviewer's Words

Each question from the interviewer should be indicated with a new line and preceded with a Q:

Example: Q: Where was the wedding held?

Edit all interviewer questions for brevity and clarity. A lengthy question may be reduced to only a few words, so long as the words chosen fully capture the main point of the question.

Do not transcribe frequently uttered supportive sounds made by the interviewer (e.g. mmm, hmm, and uh-huh).

Common listening expressions (e.g. Wow! That's unbelievable!), made by the interviewer should be transcribed.

A Final Word about Editing

Once the verbatim is complete you may want to edit the oral history for publication. The purpose of editing is not to rewrite the stories, but to help make the written version of the oral history flow well, while still retaining the personality of the interviewee. This means that the person editing an oral history must have the integrity and desire to maintain the original words and personality of the interviewee, rather than impose his or her ideas or interpretations on the story. In addition, the editor will also act as auditor or fact checker, to ensure the accuracy of the story as a whole. If an interviewee gives wrong information, which is usually unintentional and the result of a faulty memory, the editor can correct the information by adding a footnote or parenthetic statement.

Example: "We were living in a house on 4th Street in De Moines." (Editor's note: Records show the house was actually located at 609 14th Street).

Publication

Preparing the Oral History Manuscript for Publication

Publishing the manuscript is the final step in the oral history process. The finished manuscript should be neat, tidy, accurately typed and easy to read.

Before publishing, add a title page and preface to the manuscript. Typically, the title page should only carry the title of the manuscript. Using the example discussed earlier, the title page would simply read: Oral History of Mildred Ruth Campbell Beacon

The preface is intended to provide the reader with the pertinent information about the interview. As the interviewer, you are the perfect person to write the preface; as a general rule, include information about the significance and purpose of the interview, who was involved, and a statement about the original recording, verbatim, and edited manuscript.

Begin the preface with a brief introduction of the interviewee and the significance of the information he/she shares in the interview. Tell the reader why he/she should want to read the manuscript. Also add a sentence or two about why the oral history was taken and published, as well as the specific time and place that the interview occurred. Identify yourself to readers with a statement that gives your full name, your interest in the oral history, your relationship with the interviewee, and any special qualifications you may have that further explain your reasons for creating the publication. It is also important to inform readers that the manuscript is an edited version of the oral interview, and where the original tape recording and full verbatim records can be found.

Publication: Copy, Bind, Distribute!

No matter how you plan to share your oral history manuscript, it must be neatly and securely bound first. There are many quick-print shops that can copy and bind manuscripts for a very nominal price. Full books can also be printed by companies specializing in "print on demand." You'll find many reputable ones online if you simply search for "print on demand" or "POD publishing." Once you've decided where to have your manuscript printed, you may wonder how many copies you should order. Be sure to publish sufficient copies for every current member of your family. But our suggestion is to publish as many copies as you can comfortably afford, because the more copies you produce, the more likely it is that some will survive and be preserved for future generations.

The final step in your oral history project is to ensure that your manuscript is distributed to everyone who has an interest in your family history. Circulate copies to as many family members as you can think of (young and old). And don't be discouraged if some of them don't seem too interested in reading it at the present time. Someday they will. As you present it to family members, it never hurts to emphasize that it is a family treasure that is not only intended for them, but for future generations as well. As we move more and more into a digital age, you'll likely discover that some of your family members would prefer to read your oral history manuscript online. The internet is an ideal way to share your recordings, and offers a variety of ways to do so. Create a family website and upload your video and audio recordings. It's not only easy to do, but it can also be free with website that utilize Wordpress, such as www.blog.com or www. blogspot.com. With a family website everyone can view your files at any time, and can also contribute additional information, photos and family documents if they wish. If you'd like to see an example, you're welcome to visit this author's family site at www.RonaldDRoss.com.

And don't limit circulation to family members; offer a copy of your book to public libraries and historical societies as well. You just never know who, in the future, may be interested in reading about your interviewee's memories and stories.

Although you may be focused on getting your family history out to as many people as you can think of, don't forget to safeguard your materials as well. Store your disks in a safe place that does not get too much sun or cold. No one knows really how long CDs and DVD disks are going to last so be careful and keep yours away from water, heat or cold just to be safe. Don't make the common—but often disastrous—mistake of leaving you only digital copies of your audio or video files on a computer or in the recording device, assuming they will always be safe there. Technological components inevitably break down, which means that they are ultimately quite unreliable storage places for important files. Store a copy on your PC or laptop if you like, but ensure that you also have other copies stored in various other devices, such as thumb drives, off-sight web storage sites, external disk drives, etc. That way, if one device malfunctions, you haven't lost all your hard work, and irreplaceable stories. Make new copies of your recordings every 5 – 7 years. It is likely as new technology advances you will be required to upgrade your disks to the latest player files and player systems. Label clearly all original files along the following lines, "Original Oral History of Grandma Beeson Do Not Edit. Do Not Destroy."

"*The past reminds us of timeless human truths and allows for the perpetuation of cultural traditions that can be nourishing; it contains examples of mistakes to avoid, preserves the memory of alternative ways of doing things, and is the basis for self-understanding.*"
-- Drew Bettina

Chapter 8

Preserving Other Important Family History Items

Preserving your family history through recorded interviews is an excellent way of ensuring that the stories, memories, and facts will remain vivid and alive for future generations. But there are many other historically important items that belong to your family's legacy that also require careful attention and preservation. Visit any antique store, and you'll find room after room stuffed with heirlooms that at one time were likely cherished by their owners, but are now for sale to strangers who know nothing of their origin, historical meaning, or sentimental significance. Likewise, many family photos and documents are carelessly tossed in a shoe box and stored in a damp basement or hot attic. As time passes, these mementos become less significant, not only because of physical deterioration and decay, but also become those who could provide information about the people in the photos, and the stories behind them, may no longer be living.

In all likelihood, these photos, documents, and heirlooms were stored away with the best of intentions. Someone obviously cared enough to put them aside for safe keeping. Perhaps they always meant to sort, label, and preserve these treasures 'one day'—but simply never got around to it. Imagine how they'd feel if they knew that the old boxes in the attic that hold such a wealth of information about your family his-

tory would ultimately be destined for the rubbish bin, or the mantel piece of a stranger. How would you feel if that was the fate of your oral history recordings and family history manuscript?

It's human nature to think that 'someone' will take care of the things that are important to our collective family history. But why leave it to someone else, and risk not having it done at all? Why not take on the responsibility yourself, so you know for certain that your family heirlooms, photos, and documents are properly cared for and preserved? It may seem like a daunting task, but there are many excellent resources available to help you.

One that I highly recommend is a book entitled Collection, Use, and Care of Historical Photographs (Robert A. Weinstein and Larry Booth), which provides exhaustive guidance on preserving your historical items, and a realistic and common sense approach. Both new and used copies are available on Amazon. com or similar websites. The Internet is also a great source of information about literally everything; simply conduct a search for the subject you're interested in, such as "preserving photos" or "preserving antique china," and you'll have a wealth of guidance and tips at your fingertips.

What Should I Preserve?

One of the frequent questions we get from readers is, "Which family records should I preserve? After all, I can't keep *every-thing*!" This is a reasonable question, because no matter how committed you are to preserving your family's history there's a limit to how much space you can devote to storing these items.

The general rule is to keep anything that verifies who did what and when. Below you'll find some specific suggestions about the kinds of items you should attempt to preserve. As you read through this list, you may notice that we haven't mentioned photographs. That's intentional. Handling, documenting, and preserving old photos is almost an art in itself, and for that reason you'll find a very detailed discussion of how to safely store your photos in the next chapter.

In addition, there will likely be some family treasures that don't clearly fall into any of these categories, and in those cases you'll have to rely on your own good judgment. If you feel that an item has value and meaning to your family, and is (or may someday be) an heirloom, definitely document and keep it! Most often, however, the majority of your items will fit into one of the following categories, and are definite candidates for preservation.

Family Histories

You may discover that some rather extensive genealogical histories already exist for your family. If you're lucky, these will be in book form, already neatly bound. But others may be in loose-leaf binders, or even in a helter-skelter stack of pedigrees and bits of family information. Regardless of what shape they're in, these genealogies are priceless! Scan and copy all original documents, and also preserve the originals with care. Again, store copies in various places just as you did with your oral history recordings, to minimize the chances that these wonderful documents will be lost.

Another common way of documenting significant family events is a family Bible. If you're fortunate enough to have one of these, you'll want to preserve all the information! Copy out by hand or photocopy (don't remove pages) all family records found in Bibles, baby books, etc. If hand-copying, copy names and dates precisely as they are written even if they vary from other family documents. When extracting information from such a record, accurately note the source. Make other historical notes concerning the record such as who has possession of the Bible, the assumed reliability of the information and other references. Be aware, however, that not all information found in family Bibles and baby books is necessarily accurate. In going through my mother's items after her death we found an old family Bible that listed my name and birthdate, but both were wrong!

Books of Remembrance and Scrapbooks

Baby books, guest books, wedding books, anniversary memory books and other similar books of remembrance should be documented (time, place, person, etc.), saved and protected from deterioration. Scrapbooks are especially valuable historical statements. Your old Elvis Presley scrapbook may at first glance appear childish and not worth saving. However, consider how thrilled you would be to find a scrapbook kept by your great-grandmother when she was a teenager. So before you simply discard a scrapbook or other mementoes that may seem valueless to you, consider what they may be able to tell future generations about the person who created them.

Church Records

Baptismal records, marriage certificates, membership transfer letters and other official records of each family member should be carefully catalogued and preserved.

Journals, Diaries and Biographies

A diary is a written account of daily thoughts and passing events usually written with little thought for its historic significance. Any journal or diary that you or a member of your family has kept for whatever period of time should be saved. A diary kept while you were a teen may be filled with what you consider to be foolish and insignificant musings. Do not judge it by how you feel about it today, but think how your descendants will value a document that describes the thoughts, feelings and actions of an ancestor when that ancestor was a teen in the 1900s. The variety of subjects discussed in diaries will be of great interest to future generations. A diary usually includes information about health, weather, celebrities, gossip, scandal, religion, domestic life, travel, social life and more. They are wonderful pieces of the family puzzle that reveal the personality, pastimes, pursuits and invaluable insights into the world of the writer.

Old Letters

Old family letters are as valuable to your family history as clay tablets or ancient books are to historians. They provide glimpses into the hearts and minds of family members, and reveal the thoughts, concerns, challenges and actions of the writer and the recipient.

My maternal grandfather was an avid letter writer to all of his children and grandchildren. His letters revealed his strongly held opinions and distinctive personality and have been kept by all who received them. My wife saved all the love letters I sent to her the few months we were separated before our wedding. Our parents kept every letter we and our children wrote them from Africa when we lived there for seven years, and we kept the ones they sent to us. While they may not be historically significant like the Dead Sea Scrolls, to us they are priceless.

Financial Records

Often financial records are destroyed as worthless dust collectors. However, many contain information that one day may be valuable to you or your descendants. Documents on real estate purchases, receipts for payments to hospitals, mortuaries, insurance companies, clubs and other organizations should be filed for posterity. I would love to see the original documents for my grandfather's homestead in Deer Trail, Colorado. The house he built still stands but the documents verifying that he once owned it are gone. One day your children may want to peruse the papers verifying the purchase of the home they first remember.

Photographs, Movies, Video Tapes, Paintings

Today family members have the benefit of photography and videography to pass down to future generations. Photos are not very valuable, however, if no one can identify who is in the photo and when and where it was taken. Get your photos out of the shoe box in the basement and start sorting them out. Toss meaningless or unclear photos then spend some time documenting the people in the pictures you know are significant.

Home movies became popular starting in the 1950s. All home movies should be converted to digital video files by a professional service. To find one locally use the Internet and search for "video transfer services" and you'll find someone nearby with the necessary equipment.

Works of art that feature family members—or works of art done by family members—should also be carefully documented. The standard information (who, what, when where and why) should be permanently attached to the work of art in a way that will not damage the work.

Yearbooks, Atlases, Favorite Books, School Awards

High school and college yearbooks are significant historical statements that reveal styles, interests and activities of a particular year. Old atlases or maps show streets, roads and highway that one day may be torn up to make way for a super highway or shopping mall.

Ribbons, prizes, awards, diplomas, report cards and transcripts are delightful keepsakes for each family member. Keep them all.

Children and adults have favorite books. Keep them, but take the time to write a note about the book and its owner and place it inside fly leaf so that your descendants will understand its meaning and value.

Announcements

Engagement, wedding, anniversary, graduation, funeral and birthday announcements and invitations are worthy of preserving in an orderly way.

Handcrafted Items

Handcrafted items are wonderful for history lovers and often have more value and meaning than most other "hard" items you could preserve. While in college my girlfriend (now my wife) and I exchanged valentines on Valentine's Day. We didn't have any money so we agreed that we would make each other a valentine. We have preserved them for the benefit of our own memory, but they will also be available for our grandchildren to enjoy.

Household Items

Dishes, silverware, souvenirs and other such keepsakes can be handed down from one generation to the next. Each item should be documented with a written summary of its significance.

Newspaper Clippings

Announcement, obituaries, news articles and significant historical headlines are worth preserving. In our stack of newspaper clippings we have the newspaper from the day President Kennedy was assassinated as well as a news story about our family dog who liked to fly with my pilot father.

Do *not* laminate news items. Instead store them in acid-free document folders. Unfold them as much as possible (creases weaken the paper and cause it to fall apart) and store them flat. Also, avoid doing your own 'restoration' on tattered newsprint by applying glue or tape, as these substances will hasten deterioration. If possible, preserve each clipping so that the portion of the newspaper that includes the newspaper name and date of issue is visible.

Legal Papers and Licenses

Every family accumulates a variety of legal documents that will have significance for descendants. Carefully preserve last wills and testaments, deeds, titles, immigration papers, passports, adoption documents, and noteworthy leases, contracts, etc. Also to be preserved are professional and business licenses issued by various authorities. Even old drivers licenses, hunting and fishing licenses and firearms licenses will be of interest to descendants.

Employment Records

Apprenticeship records, seminar certificates, citations, retirement papers, union papers, awards, business cards, business stationery, resumes, etc. all should be filed away for posterity.

Military Records

Conscription papers, military IDs, orders, disability records, service medals, fire arms, ribbons, uniforms, citations, war souvenirs, discharge papers, etc. are worthy of archiving.

Unique Family Items

Every family has certain items that are especially relevant to their history and traditions. Preserve all special family items and fully document them as well.

Some Final Rules for Preservation

Do not experiment or improvise in preservation methods. Use only proven methods of preservation. When in doubt, ask an expert. A tremendous amount of information is available on the Internet. For instance, you can go to YouTube.com and search

"How to preserve newspaper clippings" and several videos will demonstrate how it's done.

Document, document, document! It's always better to have too much documentation rather than not enough. Just after my mother's funeral, my son went through some items and found a particular curio that he wanted. He turned it over and saw that Mom had taped his name to the bottom of it, preserving it for him. She also took the time to write out the history of a lovely silver coffee service she gave us that is now well over 100 years old – and we know its complete history. Careful documentation gives meaning and significance to family heirlooms.

And finally: don't procrastinate! Procrastination is a slippery slope that quickly leads from "I'll do that tomorrow" to "Maybe next week" to next month, next year, and ultimately, to never. Make a start today on preserving the valuable keepsakes that will mean the world to future generations tomorrow!

> *"Time will never stand still and those moments that bring us such joy become memories in an instant. To capture such a moment and record it forever is truly monumental."* -- Joshua Atticks

Chapter 9

Handling, Organizing, Documenting and Preserving Photographs

Since photography burst on the scene in 1839, families around the world have taken pictures. George Eastman, with his invention of the Brownie camera and roll-film, made picture taking common place. The ease of capturing our precious memories on camera has, unfortunately, also meant that sometimes we tend to take our photographic records for granted. And so in almost every home you can find boxes of memories simply disintegrating in basements, attics, and spare closets.

And when we do get around to looking through them, we often find ourselves wondering "Who is that with Uncle George?" "Is that Arizona or Texas? What year was this? That's Grandma, but whose house is it? Those were my best friends when I was only five years old – but I can't remember their names. Here's a really old photo – who is that, anyway? This is a picture of my old '49 Ford; how come it's all wrinkled up?"

All of these questions, of course, are asked too late. Names can't be recalled, places are forgotten, dates are unknown and history is lost. Yet, when the photo was taken, the people, place and moment were worth preserving. And for members of your family—now and future—they always will be, but only if they're properly preserved.

Family photo collections are vital to a permanent family history. Those who will never listen to a five-hour oral history will take time to glance through a photo album.

Take a moment to consider what photographs do: They verify similarities and differences of family members. They preserve important facts concerning relationships, dates, events and places. They show architecture, automobiles, pets, toys and other important family items and activities. Think of what a single photo of great-grandma dressed up for her first trip to the moving pictures could tell your descendants about her, and about your family!

This chapter provides the family historian with some guidelines for handling, categorizing, documenting and preserving the family photograph collection. These suggestions should provide you with the basic knowledge you require, but are hardly exhaustive. If you would like to consult a complete guide to the collection, care, and use of photographs we highly recommend *Collection, Use, and Care of Historical Photographs* (Robert A. Weinstein and Larry Booth), published by the American Association for State and Local History, Nashville, Tennessee (ISBN 0-910050-21-X).

How to Handle Precious Family Photos

Old photos long stored in a box in the basement are usually brittle and curled, and require gentle, careful handling. One important aspect of handling old photos is protecting them from dirt, dust, and body oils, which can scratch or otherwise permanently mark them. If you are handling them with your bare hands, wash your hands frequently. Preferably, wear cotton gloves to avoid leaving finger prints on negatives and prints alike (inexpensive disposable cotton gloves such as those that can be purchased at Walgreens are fine). Alternately, use freshly laundered soft cotton cloths such as those used for dusting.

Work on a soft surface – do not sort photos on the basement floor. Use the dining room table or other large work space, covered with a soft cotton table cloth to avoid damaging already-brittle prints.

More tips for handling your photos

- Wear cotton gloves.

- Change gloves when they become dirty.

- Handle photos with care.

- Do not expose your photos to food, liquids, glue, smoke, extended sunlight or intense artificial light.

- Do not use adhesives.

- Keep pets and children away from your photos.

- Remove all photos from those cheap self-sealing picture albums. The acid in the adhesive pages will eventually rot your photos.

- Remove all paper clips, gator clips, rubber bands, etc.

- If a photo has been glued to a page or piece of cardboard, try to remove it. Be careful in the process, however, because you can do more harm by trying to remove it than by leaving it as is. There is a handy tool called an *archival spatula* you might want to invest in.

- Digitize really important photos using a scanner.

- Store all photos flat. Do not put a folder of 3" x 5" prints stacked on top of the other, at the bottom of a stack of folders filled with 8" X 10" prints.

- Separate all photos with acid-free paper.

- Place your photos in acid free boxes or files and/or use polypropylene or Mylar sleeves.

- Number your boxes and envelopes so someone else can understand your system.

- Store in a cool, dry place. Changes in temperature and humidity can cause chemical reactions that aid deterioration.

Damaged Photos

Water damage, adhesives, tape, paper clips, temperature and other environmental factors can damage historic photos. Unless you are an expert photo restorer, do not attempt to repair damaged photos on your own. Put aside damaged photos for expert treatment, and store them separately from photos in good shape until you can locate an appropriately skilled technician (search "antique photo repair" or "photo restoration"). Personally, I use—and recommend—www.apageisturned.com for expert photo repair as well as other services related to photos and videos. Their commitment to excellence is above standard and their prices are right.

Antique Photographs

Old photographs and negatives like daguerreotypes, ambrotypes and glass-plate negatives should be placed in Mylar sleeves or in acid free, archival envelopes, and handled as little as possible. However, you may also want to consider having copies of these photos made by a reputable company, and adding the 'new' copies to your organized collection so everyone can enjoy them.

How to Organize Your Family Photo Collection

It's not always easy to sort your photos by family members of era. For instance, it's often difficult to distinguish between a 1954 photo and a 1960 one. The task can become even more complicated if you have no clue who some of the individuals in the photo with Uncle Fred are. However, there are some steps you can take that will help make preserving your photos both easier and less complicated.

1. Don't rush. It took a few generations to accumulate so many photos, so don't expect to have everything sorted and organized within an hour! Work with a few at a time. Limit your work time to 30 minutes or an hour so you don't get overwhelmed by the task.

2. Create a comfortable workspace. Get a table you can dedicate to the task and set it in a place with good lighting. A soft cotton tablecloth will help protect your photos and keep

them from sliding around. If you can leave your project in place until you are finished, so much the better.

3. Find a common sense way to separate your photos. I use large manila envelopes that I label with "David's childhood" or "Grandma & Grandpa Filatreau." You can use albums, scrapbooks or good old-fashioned shoeboxes, if you prefer, so long as the method you choose allows you to keep your photos organized. Also note that if you choose boxes or envelopes, acid-free is best.

4. Take a quick look through all of your photos in order to identify the 'keepers.' Get rid of badly blurred photos and anything that is too bright or too dark. Also, throw out photos not worthy of keeping. If you have duplicates you might want to set them aside for other family members. While you're doing this 'first pass' of your photos, also sort the ones you've decided to keep into categories corresponding to the inventory system you've decided on (Step 3). Move quickly; you needn't deliberate too long over any particular photo, as you'll be doing a second, more detailed sort later. The focus here is to simply discard the unusable photos, and impose a preliminary order and loose organization on the rest for now. Don't be tempted to skip this step, though, as it's a very important part of your process. Even if you don't

get past this stage (but you will!) at least you'll have made a first pass at organizing your family photos.

5. Work with one envelope at a time, next take a second more careful pass through the photos. Toss photos that, on second glance, don't seem relevant to your family's history such as the lovely sunset shot someone took as they drove through the California desert on their way to Disneyland. Of course, if the desert sunset shot is important to you on a personal level, by all means keep it, but store it in another spot rather than with your family history photos. As for the keepers, identify as many of the details about the photo as you can (who, what, where, when, the occasion, etc.). This will lead you to Step 6.

6. Label your photos. Record everything you know about each photo including names of each person in the photo, the date and place where the photo was taken. *Do not* use a Sharpie pen or ball-point pen to write on the backs of the photos. Use instead an archival pen or pencil. Don't know what they are? Google them and find out before writing on the back of any photo.

When using an archival pen or pencil, write in a discreet location on the back of the photo, perhaps along the edges, but always away from the important characters in the picture. Alternatively, if you put each photo inside an archival quality plastic sleeve, you can place an information card along with the photo giving all the important information you have.

7. Place in albums or other acid-free environments for preservation. Frame and display your favorites so others can enjoy them too. Pictures in envelops and boxes may never be seen. When family visitors come by, bring out the boxes and share them so everyone can enjoy them. Not only will you likely get even more information from other family members about the photos, but in sharing your family history together, you'll also be making new memories with your loved ones.

*"Genealogy becomes a mania, an ob-
sessive struggle to penetrate the past
and snatch meaning from an infinity of
names. At some point the search becomes futile – there is nothing left to
find, no meaning to be dredged out of
old receipts, newspaper articles, letters,
accounts of events that seemed so important fifty or seventy years ago. All
that remains is the insane urge to keep
looking, insane because the searcher has
no idea what he seeks. What will it be?
A photograph? A will? A fragment of a
letter? The only way to find out is to
look at everything, because it is often
when the searcher has gone far beyond
the border of futility that he finds the
object he never knew he was looking
for."* -- Henry Wiencek, The Hairstons:

An American Family in Black and White

Chapter 10

Eight Ways You Can Preserve Your Family History

1. Keep a personal journal. Write about what you do and how you feel about it. Can you imagine what a treasure it would be for you to find your grandmother's she wrote during the first few years of her marriage? The same will be true for your descendents, and the life-clarifying and self-managing benefit of journaling will be yours in the meantime.

2. Save newspaper and magazine stories with important headlines. We have the original newspaper that came out in our town the day after President Kennedy was assassinated.

Many people have preserved magazine and newspaper articles concerning the events of 9/11/2001, hurricane Katrina in August 2005, and other newsworthy events such as presidential elections.

3. Videotape your home. Here is how we have done it: I serve as the cameraman and have my wife give a tour of the home. As we walk through it she describes each room and even introduces the viewer to our pets.

4. Visit places you've lived before and photograph them. This is a wonderful and inexpensive vacation for the whole family. Take your children or grandchildren to a tour of the old home place and other places you have lived. Photograph them and create a little memory book of "homes we lived in". If you video tape the various locations you can add audio giving addresses, descriptions and remembrances. While visiting places you have lived, use your cell phone to send photos to siblings or other family members.

5. Scrapbook your family heritage. A heritage scrapbook album is a great way to protect and present family photos, heirlooms, and memories. There is an entire scrapbooking industry ready to help you create the perfect family heirloom. For help with a scrapbook, search "heritage scrapbooking" and you'll have all the help you need. It is also likely your local library has help in this area.

6. Start a family web site. Most families are online so this is a great way to get them to talk about the family, share memories, post photos and videos, exchange family recipes, tell funny stories, impart family wisdom, etc. You can do this at no cost whatsoever and with minimal web-builder experience with a variety of free website services.

7. Create a family time capsule. Pick a special day (significant wedding anniversary or birthday) and have everyone present contribute something significant (or insignificant but interesting) for placement in a box that will later be sealed with instructions NOT to be opened until a certain date. What is especially good about this project is that it can involve every member of the family no matter the age. For more on this idea search "create a family time capsule" and you'll have many ideas.

8. Document family heirlooms. Most families have what my mother called "do-dads" that, while not of real value are of great significance. For instance I have a little glass horse with a missing leg that has set on my dresser or desk since I was 5-years-old when it was given to me as a gift at my birthday party. Take a 3 X 5 index card and document such heirlooms so when your children have your estate sale these mementos are not sold for a quarter.

"Write about small, self-contained incidents that are still vivid in your memory. If you remember them, it's because they contain a larger truth that your readers will recognize in their own lives. Think small and you'll wind up finding the big themes in your family saga." -- William Knowlton Zinsser

Chapter 11

The Easy Way to Write Your Family History

Has anyone told you, "You should write the story of your life"? While it sounds like a great idea, it's not easy to do. Most writers start with their birth story and then write about their parents and siblings. After that, things get difficult and frustrating as they get lost in the minutia of what has become a massive and arduous project.

My father had the answer. He said, "I can't write my life's story, but I can write stories about my life." And he did. In his 80s he spent many hours, mostly late at night, hand-writing dozens of stories that spanned his entire life. Some were only a few paragraphs long, others were longer, and many were written as parables for the benefit of his descendents. Mother edited, typed and compiled them into three-ring binders for my brother and me to cherish.

You can do the same thing

Here is a system I developed based somewhat on my father's experience: **Write topically**. There are two ways to write topically. The first is to use lists of various items, events, activities, etc., that include sentences or short paragraphs about each subject; the second is to write stories on topics that are relevant to your life experience and important for your descendents to be aware of. You will be surprised and pleased to discover this is much easier to do and more interesting for your descendents to read than a chronological account of your life. Best of all, writing it will be more fun than you've had for years!

Here is a list of topics you can draw from or add to as you determine what you want to write about:

Lists that inform your descendents about your life:

- Places you have lived
- Interesting places you have visited
- Significant accomplishments
- The various jobs you have had over the years

- Best friends through the years

- Most interesting relatives

- Your favorite things (toys, books, furniture, gifts, etc.)

- Your favorite music through the years

- Your favorite TV shows or movies

- Favorite places to visit

- Various vehicles you have owned

- Foods you like and dislike

- The people who have most influenced your life

- Churches and clubs you joined

- Pets you have had

- Weather phenomenon you have experienced

- Technological advances you have witnessed since a youth

Interesting stories about your life:

- Your birth story

- Memories of your childhood

- Your favorite toys as a child

- Memorable family vacations

- Your views on politics

- Your views on religion

- Civic and community services you rendered

- Your brothers, sisters, aunts, uncles, cousins, and other interesting relatives

- How you met your spouse

- The day you married

- Interesting stories about your spouse

- Birth stories of each of your children

- Interesting stories about your children

- What you dreamed about as a teenager

- Things you like to collect

- Embarrassing moments in your life

- Proud moments in your life

- Secrets you kept from your spouse

- Troubles you got into over the years

- Your favorite hobbies

- Your impression of the times we live in

- Your favorite restaurants, what you like to order, and how much it costs

- Your school days

- Your first love

- Your medical problems (or lack of them) over the years

- The three biggest challenges you have faced

- Spiritual experiences you have had

- Your favorite time of the year

- Sports you've enjoyed playing or watching

- Thoughts on raising children

- Stories you remember your grandparents telling about their parents and grandparents

- Advice to your children and grandchildren

There are many, many more topics you can write about. Do not use this as a check-list, but rather a guideline and a stimulator for ideas.

Where to begin

Select five easy-to-write-about topics and complete them before going on to other topics. Your writings do not have to be exhaustive or eloquent. The easiest and most authentic way to write is to write like you talk. Sometimes only one or two sentences are sufficient.

If you write using a computer, make separate documents for each category and carefully identify them so they don't get deleted. Immediately after you complete each story, print it out and compile them all in a 3-ring binder.

If you write longhand or use a typewriter, make photo copies as a safeguard against losing them.

Editing your stories

Remember for whom you are writing! You are NOT writing with the hope of winning a Nobel Prize for Literature. You are writing so your children and grandchildren will have a record of the life you lived and the wisdom you want them to possess. Do NOT be obsessed with style, accurate punctuation, or precise paragraph formation. Perfection can be a project destroyer. Just tell the story the best way you can and let it stand.

Don't worry about absolute accuracy

Names, dates and, places are important, but not mandated. There will be times when you're not sure you have the facts right or the quotes exact, but don't worry, it's your story, so tell it like you want to.

At one stop when I was recording (video) my mother's and father's life stories, we had just finished shooting several scenes in front of the first house I remember as a child. We packed up the gear and were about to drive off when Dad said, "Ron, I've got one more story to tell." So Dad and I got back out of the car, set up the camera, and hooked up the microphone while mother sat in the car with the window open and an impatient attitude.

Once everything was ready, I signaled to Dad to start talking. He spent several minutes giving an interesting account of something that happened in the house in the background. When he was done, I shut off the camera, and then Mother spoke with a measure of disgust in her voice, "Well, Lloyd, that's not how that happened at all!"

Dad's response was quick and sure, "Aw, shut up, Loretta. It's my story and I'll tell it the way I want to." Unfortunately my camera was off and I missed what could have been a 30-second summary of their life as husband and wife.

Dad's advice is good for you: Tell your story the way YOU want to.

Your personal history grows

As you write about each topic, your fascinating life comes alive. One story builds on another, one list jogs your memory for a second, third or tenth list, each anecdote brings to life memories that will both inform and entertain your descendants. By writing stories of your life rather than your life's story, what could be a momentous task will become a joy for you to write and a treasure for your family.

Chapter 12

Give the Gift of Preserving Your Family History

By Julie Hall

Today, like any other day, I walked out to my mailbox and found an envelope from my elderly father. I can't remember receiving much mail from Dad in the past; it has always been Mom who sent me things. But it was Dad's handwriting, and I have been worried because he hasn't been well.

I opened the letter not knowing quite what to expect. Much to my surprise, I found the following letter along with a handful of photographs that had been enlarged:

Dear Julie,

I am enclosing several enlargements of old slides I found in the back of the garage. I thought you and the others that are in the photos should have them -- sorry, in some of them you weren't even born yet. It is important for you to have these because they show both sides of your family; these are the people you come from. You should preserve these and show them to your children and grandchildren, as your mother and I are doing now.

Love to all, DAD

It made me realize two things. First, our older parents do think about these things and do worry that once they are gone, all family lineage will die with them. In my estate business, I see this all too often. On the flip side, I see families that preserve almost too much and it becomes information overload for the kids. As a result, they lose interest. Is there a happy medium? I think there can be.

Secondly, as a boomer myself, I feel that many of us in our 40s, 50s, and 60s neglect to ask about our heritage until our loved ones are either infirm or pass away. I have seen so many of my boomer clients say they "wish they could talk to mom and ask who this person is in the photo."

So what can be done? It takes a little planning, but here's what I suggest:

While your parents are still living, and if you are blessed to still have grandparents living, start asking questions, have them share stories, and ask to go through photographs so you can play the game of "name that person." All too often I see heirs throwing away family photographs because they are unidentified.

The tricky part is to make sure you ask your older relatives prior to memory impairment. Once they are gone, or their memory is gone, the likelihood of someone else in the family remembering is very small.

Choose a select amount of photos that you would like to preserve and have them professionally copied for other siblings/ heirs. This is a lovely gift to give family members! Some clients of mine have actually done this and created memory books for each child, complete with "who's who" for each photo. If photos are worn, creased or damaged from time, there are services available to restore those pictures to amazing quality.

If there are too many photographs to have reproduced and it is not financially feasible to do so, use your digital camera and photograph each picture. This can be put on CDs for you and for other family members. This costs very little and takes up almost no room.

Remember: If you handle original photos, keep them in acid-free envelopes. Use a tiny post-it arrow on the back to identify who is in each photo, until you can write on your own inventory sheet, reproduction photo, or CD. Use this article from Kimberly Powell (About.com) to help you with proper scanning procedures:

http://genealogy.about.com/cs/digitalphoto/a/digital_photos. htm

It doesn't only have to be about photos. It can be your father's war items that you can have beautifully displayed in a shadow box, like the one I saw recently at a friend's house. Her father's Army photo, with his dog tags, and several other mementos looked terrific on the wall, instead of thrown in a box that won't be admired much.

Perhaps grandma never finished the quilt she was working on, and all you have are square remnants. Why not take these to a professional and have them made into pillows for the siblings? I have even seen these framed as well.

Of course, I still feel the best way to preserve family history is to give your elders the most spectacular gift of all -- yourself and some time. Spend a Sunday every few weeks and make it a point to record or video them (with permission, of course) or just write down everything they say: the funny stories, family tragedies, etc. Accumulate this precious information and create your own family book based on first-hand information.

These are just a few ideas that will help you preserve your family history. Remember, one of the biggest regrets I see is when a loved one dies and it's too late to ask questions. Take a little time with a loved one, make their day, and learn about where you came from!

© 2010, The Estate Lady Used with permission

Julie Hall, known as The Estate Lady, is a professional estate liquidator and certified personal property appraiser. With more than eighteen years experience, she has assisted thousands of individuals in the daunting and often painful process of managing their deceased parents' affairs. http://www.theestatelady.com

She has authored a best-selling book titled "THE BOOMER BURDEN: How to Deal With Your Parents' Lifetime Accumulation of Stuff". Her latest book, "A Boomer's Guide to Cleaning Out Your Parents' Estate in 30 Days or Less" is a practical, take-along guide with worksheets and lists. Together, these two books will guide loved ones on how to appropriately handle their parents' belongings while keeping one's sanity...and that is priceless. Both are available on Amazon.com.

Julie writes a weekly blog at http://estatelady.wordpress.com, called The Estate Lady Speaks. Article Source: http://EzineArticles.com/?expert=Julie_Hall

Article Source: http://EzineArticles.com/4822414

Afterword:

"And I will make every effort to see that after my departure you will always be able to remember these things." -- St. Peter (2 Peter 1:15)

"The kind of ancestors we have had is not as important as the kind of descendents our ancestors have." -- Unknown

Bibliography

The following are five excellent books on oral history taking and family history preservation.

LoVerde, Mary, *Touching Tomorrow*. New York: Simon & Schuster, 2000.

Fletcher, William, *Recording Your Family History*. Berkeley, CA: Ten Speed Press, 1989.

Spence, Linda, *Legacy: A Step-by-Step Guide to Writing Personal History*. Athens, OH, Swallow Press, 1997.

Hart, Cynthia and Samson, Lisa, *The Oral History Workshop*. New York: Workman Publishing, 2009.

Franco, Carol and Lineback, Kent, *The Legacy Guide: Capturing the Facts, Memories, and Meaning of Your Life*. New York: Tarcher/Penquin, 2006.

Many other books too numerous to mention are available on the various subjects of oral history taking, transcribing and editing oral history, writing a personal oral history, preserving documents, photos, videos, and heirlooms.

To find more on any subject related to family history, search the topic in your library, your favorite search engine, or Amazon.com. Another good source for "how to" videos on the various subjects, visit YouTube.com and search your subject of interest.